Praise for *Turn Small Talk into Big Deals*

"Three of the many super tips I got from Don Gabor's *Turn Small Talk into Big Deals* were how to develop great ice breakers—I always have trouble with that first sentence; extricating myself tactfully from time wasters, which is a perennial problem; and requesting a guest list to a dinner in advance, which is a simple suggestion that never occurred to me. This book is a must-read for anyone wanting to improve their techniques gaining new relationships."

—Edward Mendlowitz, CPA, partner, WithumSmith+Brown

"People are always amazed as to why I have such a high in-person cold call success rate. My secret is using Don Gabor's first impressions and small-talk techniques. From the gatekeeper to the CEO, Don is with me. It's great stuff, and I use it daily."

—Richard J. Burgess, senior vice president, Commercial Banking–Long Island and Queens JP Morgan Chase Bank, N.A.

"Don Gabor is a wonderful resource for anyone who needs to learn to network conversationally and for those entrepreneurs who are embarking on public speaking. Don has a gift of teaching his readers and clients not only how to turn a phrase but also how to turn a new acquaintance into a business colleague. For those new entrepreneurs who are about to embark on public speaking, Don can give you the mental and physical preparation for a presentation. His real gift is the gift of courage to speak out and be heard."

—Julie Azuma, president and founder of Different Roads to Learning

"Don Gabor is the master of small talk and networking. His pithy networking tips are a favorite with Steady Elevation members, and this book offers a thorough treatment of how to network with other people, taking their natural conversational style into consideration. Brilliantly logical, yet practical and simple; building rapport and cementing relationships is no longer the hit-or-miss proposition it used to be. This is stuff every business owner, salesperson, and entrepreneur should be attuned to. I highly recommend it!"

—Meny Hoffman, founder of Steady Elevation

"Don Gabor's book *Turn Small Talk into Big Deals* takes networking to a new level! This well-thought-out, easy-to-understand book makes it an excellent resource for making strong business connections in any situation."

—Ivy Naistadt, executive speaking coach and author of *Speak Without Fear, a Total System for Becoming a Natural, Confident Communicator*

"If you want to be a better networker, take your business to the next level, and make a lot more sales, especially the *big* ones, then buy Don Gabor's book, *Turn Small Talk into Big Deals*. It's a winner, and after reading it, you will be, too!"

—Stephan Schiffman, author of 49 books, including *Cold Calling Techniques: (That Really Work!)*

"Don Gabor is a genius when it comes to small talk and big results. Understanding how you communicate and how it is received is critical to your success in closing big deals. If there was one person I would want to lean on for this critical information, it is Don Gabor. This book is a must-read."

—Ron Karr, CSP, author, *Lead, Sell or Get Out of the Way*

"If anyone knows how to effectively turn our words into the big deals, it's Don Gabor. He's a proven communicator."

—Audra Lowe, talk show host from *BetterTV*

TURN

small
talk

into BIG
DEALS

Also by Don Gabor

Books

Big Things Happen When You Do the Little Things Right

How to Start a Conversation and Make Friends

How to Talk to the People You Love

Speaking Your Mind in 101 Difficult Situations

Talking with Confidence for the Painfully Shy

Words That Win: What to Say to Get What You Want

Audiobooks

Cómo Iniciar una Conversación

How to Meet People and Make Friends at Work

How to Start a Conversation

Talking with Confidence for the Painfully Shy

TURN

small
talk

into **BIG**
DEALS

Using 4 Key Conversation Styles to
Customize Your Networking Approach,
Build Relationships, and Win More Clients

DON GABOR

New York Chicago San Francisco Lisbon London Madrid Mexico City
Milan New Delhi San Juan Seoul Singapore Sydney Toronto

The **McGraw·Hill** Companies

1 2 3 4 5 6 7 8 9 0 DOC/DOC 0 1 0 9

ISBN 978-0-07-159965-8
MHID 0-07-159965-7

McGraw-Hill books are available at special quantity discounts to use as premiums and sales promotions, or for use in corporate training programs. To contact a representative, please visit the Contact Us pages at www.mhprofessional.com.

This book is printed on acid-free paper.

Library of Congress Cataloging-in-Publication Data

Gabor, Don.
  Turn small talk into big deals : using 4 key conversation styles
to customize your networking approach, build relationships,
and win more clients / by Don Gabor.
      p. cm.
  Includes index.
  ISBN 0-07-159965-7 (alk. paper)
  1. Conversation. 2. Businese networks. 3. Social networks.
4. Interpersonal relations I. Title.

BJ2121.G34 2009
650.1'3—dc22   2008043958

CONTENTS

IF YOU USE A "ONE-SIZE-FITS-ALL" APPROACH TO NETWORKING, YOU MAY BE MISSING PROFITABLE CONNECTIONS WITH THREE OUT OF EVERY FOUR PEOPLE YOU MEET

I start my networking class by peeling off my sport coat. I hold it up to one fellow about my size in the group and ask him, "Do you think my sport coat will fit you?" "Maybe," he says. I move to another attendee and ask the group again, "How about this woman? Will my sport coat fit her?" People shake their heads no. "Now, what about this big guy? He looks like he was a football player in high school. Is my sport coat going to fit him?" Since I'm about 145 pounds soaking wet, the audience laughs and says, "No way!"

Of course, for most of us one-size-fits-all does not work very well when we buy clothes. Yet, many businesspeople use a one-size-fits-all approach when it comes to networking. If that's your approach, too, then I believe you are missing profitable connections with three out of every four prospects, whether you mingle at association meetings, trade shows, holiday office parties, or even online at social networking sites.

INCREASE YOUR ODDS OF CONNECTING WITH POTENTIAL CUSTOMERS

The objective of *Turn Small Talk into Big Deals* is to increase your odds of connecting with prospects and clients wherever you find them. By quickly identifying and adapting to an individual's particular conversation and networking style, anyone can instantly establish rapport and build a connection with those they meet in business, social, and public situations. In this book, I don't just tell you what to do, I show you how to do it. This practical guide will teach you how to:

- Identify and adapt to four networking styles
- Break the ice, make small talk, and network in business, social, and public situations
- Apply different etiquette for networking in business, social, and public situations
- Make business contacts on social networks
- Define networking objectives and save time
- Target "big-deal" clients and customers
- Avoid common networking mistakes
- Build instant rapport with everyone you meet
- Increase your visibility and professional image at networking events
- Overcome shyness and be confident at networking events
- Avoid people who waste your time at networking events
- Persuasively pitch "big deals" to prospective clients or customers

THIS BOOK WILL HELP YOU NETWORK AND CONNECT WITH EVERYONE—EVERYWHERE

Let's face it, everyone likes to do things his or her own way, so that's why Part I: Identifying Networking Styles and Breaking the Ice begins with identifying your own networking style. You might be surprised what you learn about your personal style of networking—your strengths, weaknesses, preferences, and motivations. Once you know your networking style, then I will show you how to identify, tune in to, and connect with the networking styles of others. This alone will improve your ability to network, connect, and make lasting business relationships, but I don't stop there. Throughout the entire book, I connect all the strategies, tips, and examples to each of the four networking styles. If you are a bit hesitant about all this mixing and mingling, don't worry because I've also included hundreds of conversation tips throughout the book.

Part II: Connecting Online and Working the Room to Find Big Deals presents eight concise communication skills–based chapters. Starting with prospecting for business on social networks, these chapters include strategies to work a room and uncover business opportunities. In addition, you'll learn ways to use a guest list to meet the right people and remember names, as well as tips for joining other conversations, guiding informal conversations to business topics, and tactfully escaping networkers who waste your time. Finally, this part reveals follow-up strategies that will turn acquaintances into business relationships and addresses common networking mistakes and how to correct them.

In Part III: Business Situations: Opening Lines, Topics, and Networking Strategies, Part IV: Social Situations: Opening Lines, Topics, and Networking Strategies, and Part V: Public Situations: Opening Lines, Topics, and Networking Strategies you will find a dozen rules of networking etiquette, 30 typical networking situations, and ways of locating topic-related social networks, plus hundreds of conversation topics, opening lines, tips, and strategies. Each of the 30 situations ends with "Taboo Topics," so you also will learn what *not* to talk about when networking.

A STRATEGIC NETWORKING PHILOSOPHY: HELP OTHERS SUCCEED AND YOU TOO WILL REAP REWARDS

The beauty of strategic networking is that everyone you meet is a potential networking contact, although you may or may not become each other's client or customer. I always approach new contacts with the attitude that if I can help them achieve their goals then, hopefully, they or someone they know will do the same for me.

This philosophy stems from a deeper belief that what a person gives in life, he or she gets back—though not necessarily from the same person. For example, sometimes the person I introduce to a potential client will return the favor. Other times, a referral for coaching or a workshop may come from someone a step or two removed from that person or from a completely different source who knows of me or has read one of my books. That is why I always find it rewarding to talk with people and discover where our goals, lives, and businesses intersect. So, if you are ready to connect with others and get some rewards of your own, then turn the page and begin *Turn Small Talk into Big Deals.*

PART I

IDENTIFYING NETWORKING STYLES AND BREAKING THE ICE

1

Identifying Your
Natural Networking Style

In this chapter you will:

- **Answer 16 questions related to how you network**
- **Determine your natural networking style**
- **Define three other networking styles**
- **Learn what motivates each networking style**

Did you know that everyone has his or her own natural style of networking—a way of reaching out to people and making connections? We don't learn it in school, but rather through experience of what has worked for us over the years.

Being able to identify and understand the networking styles of people you meet is an extremely useful communication skill. It will enhance your ability to connect with and adapt to people in any networking situation. However, before you can identify and understand what motivates others, you first must determine *your* own natural networking style.

IDENTIFYING YOUR NATURAL NETWORKING STYLE

Answer the following questions and then follow the instructions to learn your natural networking style. There are no right or wrong answers, or good or bad networking styles, so just choose the answer that best describes how you would react in each given situation.

1. When I'm networking, I prefer to engage in conversations that are
   ▲ fun and friendly.
   ■ about deep, serious topics.
   ● lively and challenging.
   ◆ calm and insightful.

2. When I network, I tend to
   ● talk about my company's great products or services.
   ◆ listen for the other person's needs and help the person connect with others.
   ▲ chat about our mutual role in the business world.
   ■ discuss the latest technologies or advancements in my industry.

3. When I meet a competitor at a networking event, I
   ■ try to find out some "inside information" about his or her company.
   ◆ compare notes about recent industry issues.
   ● debate differences about our products and services.
   ▲ discuss topics other than business.

4. When I attend networking events, I usually
   - ■ sit quietly alone and read the agenda while I wait for the program to begin.
   - ◆ find people I already know and chat with them.
   - ▲ take a seat beside strangers and engage them in conversation.
   - ● sit next to the most important people in the organization and talk to them.

5. Before I attend networking events, I
   - ● call the host of the organization for a guest list.
   - ◆ think about what I'm going to say to the people I meet.
   - ■ read up on the latest industry news.
   - ▲ ask a friend to go along with me.

6. When I network with a potential customer or client, I
   - ● push hard to convince him or her that my company's product or service is the best.
   - ▲ make small talk before guiding the conversation to a business topic.
   - ◆ listen for ways to help solve particular business problems.
   - ■ explain in detail how my company's products or services work.

7. When I network with someone who is probably not a potential client, I
   - ● quickly end the conversation and look for someone else to talk to.
   - ▲ find out who else he or she knows at the event.
   - ■ try to convince him or her to use my company's products or services.
   - ◆ look for areas of mutual interest outside of work.

8. If I see a group of people engaged in conversation across the room, I
   - ● move closer and listen to their conversation.
   - ■ remain where I am and wait for someone to come talk to me.
   - ▲ walk over and join them.
   - ◆ find another "unattached" person to talk to.

9. If I see a distinguished guest or potential client talking to a competitor, I join the conversation to
   - ● debate my opponent.
   - ▲ get to know each of them better.
   - ◆ listen for areas of mutual interest.
   - ■ tell them everything I can about my product or service.

10. After attending a networking event, I usually follow up only
    - ◆ with the people who asked me to call them.
    - ▲ with anyone who seemed nice.
    - ■ when I have time.
    - ● with the people who I think are the best prospects.

11. When I hear a speaker present a viewpoint I disagree with, I
    - ● dismiss many of the other points in the presentation.
    - ◆ listen carefully to how I can adapt the information to what I do.
    - ■ challenge the opinion during the presentation.
    - ▲ discuss his or her views with my colleagues.

12. When I'm at a networking event, I usually
    - ◆ talk to my colleagues more than anyone else.

▲ introduce myself to as many people in the room as I can.

■ find one or two people who share my interests.

● target potential clients or customers.

13. If I meet a potential client or customer who wants to do business with me, I

◆ seek more information about his or her problems or challenges.

● immediately suggest an appointment for a follow-up meeting.

▲ invite him or her to lunch to discuss working together in more detail.

■ offer detailed suggestions on how to solve the problems he or she has told me about.

14. If I see someone I've met before, but I've forgotten his or her name, I

▲ reintroduce myself and start the conversation.

◆ ask someone else who might know the person's name.

■ avoid talking to him or her out of embarrassment.

● engage him or her in conversation without using his or her name.

15. When I meet someone at a networking event who talks a lot, I

◆ quietly wait until he or she finishes.

▲ politely interrupt to offer my views and move the conversation closer to a conclusion.

● quickly end the conversation and go find someone else to talk to.

■ listen for inconsistencies and bring them up.

16. When I meet someone at a networking event who talks very little, I

    ▲ keep the conversation going by talking more.

    ● quickly end the conversation and go find someone else to talk to.

    ◆ gently ask for his or her views on industry issues.

    ■ ask a complicated question.

Interpretation

In the spaces below, write the total number of times your answer matched the symbols shown. For example, if 7 of your answers were followed with ●, 3 with ▲, 2 with ◆ and 4 with ■, then your chart will look like the sample score.

Sample score:

● __7__ Competitive Networking Style

▲ __3__ Outgoing Networking Style

◆ __2__ Amiable Networking Style

■ __4__ Analytical Networking Style

Your score:

● _____ Competitive Networking Style

▲ _____ Outgoing Networking Style

◆ _____ Amiable Networking Style

■ _____ Analytical Networking Style

Each of these symbols (●, ▲, ◆, or ■) represents one of four networking styles. Here are the key points to help you interpret what the numbers mean:

- The style with the greatest number of answers is your natural networking style.
- The style with the least number of answers is the networking style *least* like your own.

- The higher the number, the more dominant your style. The lower the number, the less dominant your style.
- If any of the networking styles have close or equal numbers, see which one best describes your strengths and weaknesses when you talk to people at networking events.
- Your networking style can shift between related styles depending on the situation you are in and to whom you are speaking.
- Some of the characteristics of the networking styles overlap.

SNAPSHOTS OF THE FOUR NETWORKING STYLES

You will meet many people in business and social situations with networking styles similar, different, or even contrary to your own. The most effective way to engage these individuals is to quickly adapt your networking style to best fit theirs. As you read about the characteristics, strengths, and weaknesses of these networking styles, see which ones describe you best.

Don't be surprised when several of your networking characteristics, strengths, and weaknesses fall into more than one style. That's natural, because no one has just one style. However, you will most likely see your characteristics fall into one primary networking style. Whatever the case, you will improve your ability to connect and network if you build on your strengths as you eliminate your weaknesses. In addition, with practice and careful observation and listening, you can begin to identify the networking styles of others within the first few minutes of your meeting and conversation. Once you have a sense of a person's style, you can adapt your own style to make the best of the conversation.

● Competitive Networking Style

Competitive Networkers are action-oriented and direct communicators, motivated by fast and measurable results. Confident and outgoing, they are usually the ones who start conversations at networking events because they don't want to waste one minute waiting for somebody else to make the first move. They speak with purpose and get to the point. They enjoy talking about their company's products and services, and how much better they are than their competitors. Without hesitation, they will debate anyone who challenges them or says otherwise.

Never let it be said that they are shy about letting others know about their recent accomplishments! Competitive Networkers expect the people they meet to talk as fast as they do and to follow along whenever they change topics. Typically, people in positions of authority, such as high-ranking sales executives, business owners, industry leaders, and entrepreneurs network in this style.

▲ Outgoing Networking Style

Outgoing Networkers are people-oriented and friendly communicators, motivated by recognition and personal contact. They love to make small talk while they effortlessly mix and mingle in business and social situations. To these natural communicators there's no such thing as a stranger because they make friends so quickly.

Outgoing Networkers are optimistic, affectionate, and warm individuals who easily connect with just about everyone they meet at networking events. They quickly build rapport with strangers, know how to win people over, and make even the shyest networkers feel more comfortable by creating a sense of trust.

Outgoing Networkers look for the positive in people and focus on what they can do—not what they can't do. Typically, people whose jobs require them to work face-to-face with other people, such as sales, teaching, human resources, public relations, customer service, and advertising, network in this style.

◆ Amiable Networking Style

Amiable Networkers are emotion-oriented and caring communicators, motivated by personal loyalty and teamwork. They are generally detail- and goal-oriented people, who work hard to achieve high standards for themselves and others. You can tell when you meet somebody with this networking style in business or social situations because they frequently use words such as "we," "us," and "our team" when they discuss projects or experiences.

While Amiable Networkers are typically reserved and soft-spoken, they are usually friendly and open to meeting new people if someone else initiates the conversation. They can appear shy early on in the conversation but will participate freely once they feel comfortable about the people with whom they are speaking.

Amiable Networkers are team players and prefer to network with others who are similarly oriented toward achieving success for their departments. They rarely claim credit for themselves, but are more likely to bestow it on individuals whom they like and respect. People who work in groups and teams, such as managers, editors, social workers, nurses, counselors, psychologists, and office assistants, often fall into this category of networkers.

■ Analytical Networking Style

Analytical Networkers are extremely detail-oriented and careful speakers who are motivated by accuracy and strive for deeper meaning and understanding in conversations. They approach conversations at networking events in the same way they do the other things in their lives—by paying close attention to facts and logic, and above all, by being correct. As a result, they communicate in a systematic, step-by-step manner, making sure they thoroughly cover each point they make.

Analytical Networkers consider networking an arduous task because it requires making small talk, which they often think of as boring and a waste of time. They prefer one-on-one conversations about more weighty topics centered on their work. They tend to avoid groups where people appear to know one another and are talking about lighter, more informal topics. Analytical Networkers typically describe themselves as perfectionists and often work in technical fields, including professions such as engineering, accounting, medicine, law, architecture, computer programming, and chemistry.

In this chapter you identified your own natural style of networking and how you prefer to converse in social and business situations. Of course, while we each have a particular networking style, we also exhibit many characteristics associated with one or more of the other styles. For this reason, it can be challenging to pinpoint a stranger's networking style right away. However, as you will read in the following chapters, the more you know about the specific communication characteristics of all the networking styles, the faster and easier it will be to build rapport and connect with others.

2

Breaking the Ice and Networking with Competitive Networkers

In this chapter you will learn:

- **Characteristics and conversational traits of Competitive Networkers**
- **Communication strengths and weaknesses of Competitive Networkers**
- **Special tips to break the ice with Competitive Networkers**
- **How to adapt your conversations to Competitive Networkers**

COMMUNICATION STRENGTH OF COMPETITIVE NETWORKERS

If you are a Competitive Networker, you are a goal-oriented person who speaks plainly, gets to the point, and quickly rises to a challenge. People like to network with you because you do what you say and say what you do. Here are a couple of additional communication strengths that characterize Competitive Networkers.

Competitive Networkers Focus on Big Ideas, Big Goals, and Big Bucks

People with a competitive style of networking are usually "big-picture" talkers and thinkers. Their conversations tend to focus more on big concepts than on the small details. At networking events, they love to talk about and discuss their big plans, past big results, and future big deals. They don't like to get into specifics. Competitive Networkers are creative people with vision. They want to be the first to capitalize on and sell an idea or a product. They value innovation when it can be proven that there is a return on investment (ROI). Because they are risk takers, they embrace challenges and love to talk about overcoming difficulties and adversity to achieve big results.

Direct Communicators Focus on the Bottom Line

"I'm a bottom-line guy—just tell me how this software will help me increase my sales." I overheard a Competitive Networker say

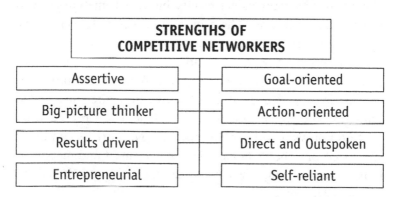

STRENGTHS OF COMPETITIVE NETWORKERS	
Assertive	Goal-oriented
Big-picture thinker	Action-oriented
Results driven	Direct and Outspoken
Entrepreneurial	Self-reliant

this to a vendor at a recent meeting. People with the competitive networking style get right to the point and want to talk about the return on investment for their time and money. Once they have enough facts, they quickly make up their minds and are not shy about telling others what they think about an idea or issue. They have strong views, particularly, about business issues and ways of getting things done.

COMMUNICATION WEAKNESSES OF COMPETITIVE NETWORKERS

If you are a Competitive Networker, you are an "all business" person who has little tolerance for people who take too long to make their point, get things done, avoid commitment, or try to please everyone around them. As a result of their often curt communication style, Competitive Networkers can intimidate others. Here are a couple of additional communication weaknesses that characterize Competitive Networkers.

Competitive Networkers Can Appear Blunt, Unemotional, and Arrogant

Competitive Networkers get results, but they sometimes offend others along the way. Their overriding desire to get to the point in the conversation can come across as blunt or insensitive. As a result, they give the impression that they lack consideration of others when they speak. Without hesitation or considering the impact of their words, they offer unsolicited criticism, ask embarrassing questions, and tell people what they do not want to hear. Competitive Networkers can make snap decisions about the people that they meet and may overlook others' feelings when discussing results and making business decisions.

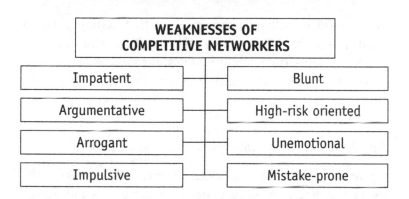

Their Aggressive Nature Can Intimidate and Offend Others

Competitive Networkers often intimidate people who have a less aggressive communication style. As a result of their aggressiveness, they can make others feel uncomfortable discussing business or other topics. Competitive Networkers can become loud, angry, and argumentative if challenged, criticized, or accused of making mistakes. Competitive Networkers often only listen for what they want to hear, thus ignoring information, details, and outcomes that do not fit into their plans or move them closer to their ultimate goals.

SIX TIPS FOR BETTER NETWORKING WITH COMPETITIVE NETWORKERS

Use the following communication strategies and see fast results when talking to people with a competitive networking style.

Tip #1: Get to the Point—Fast!

Don't waste time with long stories, background information, detailed explanations, or complicated instructions. Use the age-old method of selling newspapers by first stating a boldly worded headline. Then follow the headline with the most important supporting details and nothing more unless you are asked for it. The rule of giving information to a competitive networker is "Less is more."

Tip #2: Do Not Let a Conversation Turn into a Debate

Competitive Networkers are eager to match wits and skills with the people they meet because they look at business and conversation as a game of winning and losing. They love competition, but hate to lose, so pick your contests wisely. If you win in a golf or tennis match, you probably won't have a problem. However if you press an argument too much to win a discussion point at a networking event—even if you are right—you may lose the opportunity to pursue a big deal.

Tip #3: Focus on the Results—Not on the Process

Remember that Competitive Networkers are bottom-line people, so discuss your big deal in terms of benefits and outcomes— that is, how it can save time, increase profit, or boost efficiency. Do not explain the process of how you will achieve these goals until you present a specific proposal for a big deal. Keep your explanations short and simple if Competitive Networkers ask, "So how are you going to do that?"

Tip #4: Praise Their Prior Achievements and Visions

Competitive Networkers love to hear praise about their past achievements. They see themselves as visionaries. Your enthusiastic praise will boost their self-confidence and will make them like you and seriously consider doing business with you. As a result, they will want to learn more about how your big deal will enhance their image, position, and success.

Tip #5: Check for Understanding and Agreement

Because Competitive Networkers are not detail- or process-oriented listeners or speakers, it is useful to check for understanding at key points in a discussion. When you hear them speak in generalities about goals, outcomes, and processes, ask for specific examples of key points, objectives, and expectations. Finally, give them an executive summary of your conversation and ask for approval with, "Is that correct?"

Tip #6: Don't Be Intimidated by a Competitive Networker's Abrupt Demeanor

The trick in networking with Competitive Networkers is not to be put off by their sometimes unfriendly body language, blunt responses, or no-nonsense manner. More often than not, their gruff exterior is really a "confidence test" they like to put others through to see a response. Never defend or get defensive over a challenging remark. Instead, ask an open-ended "bottom-line" or "big-idea" question that allows Competitive Networkers to elaborate on recent accomplishments or endeavors.

COMPETITIVE NETWORKERS FREQUENTLY MAKE BIG DEALS

In this chapter you've learned about the communication strengths and weaknesses of Competitive Networkers and that being direct is the best way to engage them for a productive result. If you are a Competitive Networker you now know that at times if you present a less aggressive image and approach, Amiable and Analytical Networkers will be more open to you. If you communicate with Competitive Networkers without turning your conversations into contests, they can be among your strongest business allies.

3

Breaking the Ice and Networking with Outgoing Networkers

In this chapter you will learn:

- Characteristics and conversational traits of Outgoing Networkers
- Communication strengths and weaknesses of Outgoing Networkers
- Special tips to break the ice with Outgoing Networkers
- How to adapt your conversations to Outgoing Networkers

COMMUNICATION STRENGTHS OF OUTGOING NETWORKERS

If you are an Outgoing Networker, you like to talk and meet people anywhere, anytime. People enjoy networking with you because you are casual, lighthearted, and you make them feel comfortable and welcome in conversations. Here are some other communication strengths associated with Outgoing Networkers.

*Outgoing Networkers Are Friendly and Open
to Contact*

Outgoing Networkers are persuasive, yet not too pushy. They
enjoy influencing others and selling big deals using their passion
and enthusiasm, not pressure, logic, or overly detailed plans.
They are good networkers because they can quickly describe the
features and benefits of their products and services in simple
terms without making it sound like a canned sales pitch.

Fun to Network With and Eager to Help

Outgoing Networkers enjoy chatting one-on-one or in groups in
business and social situations. In one-on-one conversations,
their warmth makes you feel like an old friend. In groups, their
"the more the merrier" attitude creates lively and spontaneous
conversations. They strive for the greatest possible number of
personal contacts who will listen to their stories, laugh at their
jokes, and pat them on the back. In return, people like to network with them because they are fun to talk to and make an
effort to help others connect for mutual benefit.

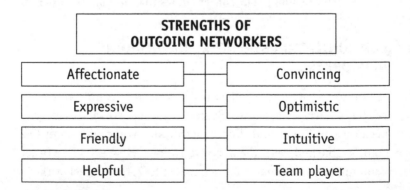

STRENGTHS OF OUTGOING NETWORKERS	
Affectionate	Convincing
Expressive	Optimistic
Friendly	Intuitive
Helpful	Team player

Follow "Gut Feelings" Over Logic

Outgoing Networkers prefer to discuss topics in terms of concepts, ideas, and feelings. Through small talk, reading between the lines of conversation, and listening for implied meanings, they get a "gut feeling" about the people they meet. Because they are confident in their ability to build rapport and connect with prospects, they can communicate the benefits of a big deal without going into great detail about the features or processes.

COMMUNICATION WEAKNESSES OF OUTGOING NETWORKERS

While Outgoing Networkers have little trouble breaking the ice, they can dominate conversations by talking too much. Although their nature is to please and win the approval of others, Outgoing Networkers can leave the impression that they prefer the sound of their own voice, thus leaving others feeling ignored or bored. Here are some more communication weaknesses associated with Outgoing Networkers.

Too Much Time Spent Socializing—Not Enough Time Spent Prospecting

Outgoing Networkers can waste time socializing at networking events with coworkers and colleagues instead of prospecting for new customers. They make the incorrect assumption that just being friendly, popular, and a good talker will lead them to new customers. They tend to rely on their natural ability to communicate and connect instead of preparing ahead of time to target specific prospects and set networking goals.

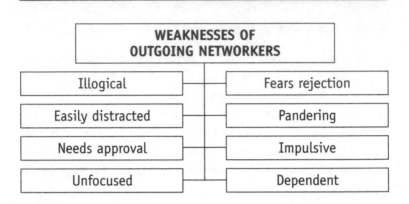

WEAKNESSES OF OUTGOING NETWORKERS	
Illogical	Fears rejection
Easily distracted	Pandering
Needs approval	Impulsive
Unfocused	Dependent

Hogging the Conversation Turns Off Less Talkative Networkers

Outgoing Networkers who talk too much can easily over-whelm and turn off others at networking events. By monopolizing the conversation, they bore others and make them feel trapped and uncomfortable. Constant interruptions by an Outgoing Networker indicate poor listening skills and a lack respect for others that greatly diminishes business opportunities.

Lack of Focus on Details Leads to Many Mistakes

Many Outgoing Networkers do not listen carefully enough for facts, instructions, dates, and other important information. Easily distracted by other activities or people, they can miss, confuse, misunderstand, or overlook important details, especially when discussing key elements of a big deal. This lack of attention to detail inevitably leads to embarrassing mistakes or missteps that can undermine their credibility.

SIX TIPS FOR BETTER NETWORKING WITH OUTGOING NETWORKERS

Tip #1: Be Personable, Friendly, and Conversational

Take time to engage Outgoing Networkers in small talk. They need to establish rapport and get to know you before they feel comfortable talking business. As you chat, encourage them to talk about themselves. (It won't be hard!) Laugh at their jokes—remember they seek the approval of others, and your laughter is a sign that they amuse you. Use big-picture concepts to describe outcomes and talk at about the same speed as they do.

Tip #2: Show Appreciation and Recognition

Ask Outgoing Networkers to describe any recent successful projects or deals. "I'd love to hear more about your . . . " is music to an Outgoing Networker's ears. Show interest and enthusiasm by asking for more details about their projects. Paraphrase what they say and reflect their feelings and attitudes about the project by restating some of the words you hear. Reinforce their attitudes about their abilities by describing their efforts in terms of fun and teamwork. Congratulate them on their accomplishments and show an interest in helping them get more recognition.

Tip #3: Express a Desire to Work Together in the Future

Outgoing Networkers usually love to work with others. Ask for ideas and brainstorm together. Once you offer a possible idea for a big deal, ask for their opinions and feedback. Encourage them to build on and expand their self-images as creative thinkers with compliments such as "What a great idea!" or "You're a real idea person!" Plant the seeds for future big projects by saying, "I can see you are fun to work with!"

Tip #4: Keep Your Comments Positive

Because Outgoing Networkers desire the approval of others, they are quickly offended by criticism or negativity, which they take personally. Focus on the positive and what will work. Emphasize the benefits of achieving specific goals and how their lives and those of their friends will improve as a result. Avoid criticizing or negating an idea, even if you know or think it won't work. Never argue or get bogged down in minor details.

Tip #5: Encourage Attention to Detail and Check for Accuracy

If you gently encourage Outgoing Networkers to pay closer attention to the details of your conversations, chances are they will improve their ability to listen for and accurately retain information. Suggest they take notes or offer them a brief written outline of your key points so that you know they have the correct information. You can also ask Outgoing Networkers to restate your main points so that you can check for understanding and correct any mistakes or misunderstandings.

Tip #6: Don't Let Outgoing Networkers Overwhelm You into Silence

The trick to networking with overtalkative Outgoing Networkers is to first interrupt them and then guide the conversations so that there will be a balance between talking and listening. Listen carefully for brief pauses in their soliloquies, and then quickly inject several closed-ended questions in a row. Outgoing Networkers will then stop, listen, and offer appropriate responses. Next, without waiting for a pause, interrupt again to offer your ideas and opinions. If Outgoing Networkers start speaking before you complete your point, politely say with a friendly smile, "Please let me finish."

OUTGOING NETWORKERS CAN BECOME YOUR BIGGEST BUSINESS BOOSTERS

In this chapter you learned that building relationships and gaining approval are big motivators for Outgoing Networkers. In addition to identifying their communication strengths and weaknesses, you now know how to engage them for a productive result. If you are an Outgoing Networker, you've learned which of your communication characteristics others consider most endearing and those that they would rather see and hear less of. Show Outgoing Networkers positive attention and reinforce their skills and achievements, and they can become your most enthusiastic business and networking associates.

4

Breaking the Ice and Networking with Amiable Networkers

In this chapter you will learn:

- Characteristics and conversational traits of Amiable Networkers
- Communication strengths and weaknesses of Amiable Networkers
- Special tips to break the ice with Amiable Networkers
- How to adapt your conversations to Amiable Networkers

COMMUNICATION STRENGTHS OF AMIABLE NETWORKERS

If you are an Amiable Networker, you are friendly, yet slightly reserved when it comes to breaking the ice with others in business and social situations. Once you get into a conversation, people like talking with you because you are nonthreatening, warm, and engaging. Here are some other communication strengths associated with Amiable Networkers.

Amiable Networkers Are Accommodating Team Players

Above all, Amiable Networkers are helpful individuals who focus more on the needs of others than on their own needs. Amiable Networkers go out of their way to introduce you to others at a networking event. Although they can be reserved in the early stages of a conversation, within a short time they feel more comfortable talking and opening up. You can count on Amiable Networkers to serve as hosts and volunteers for networking events. And since they are great team players, they always share credit for achieving big goals.

Active Listeners Come Up with Solutions

Amiable Networkers use their excellent listening skills at networking events to help sort out the big concepts along with the details necessary to achieve specific goals. Because Amiable Networkers are process oriented, other people at networking events like to share their challenges with them and then listen to their possible solutions.

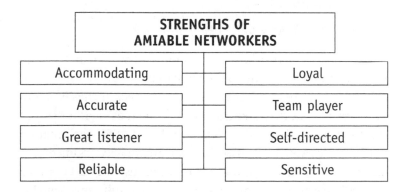

STRENGTHS OF AMIABLE NETWORKERS	
Accommodating	Loyal
Accurate	Team player
Great listener	Self-directed
Reliable	Sensitive

Loyal and Enthusiastic Advocates

Amiable Networkers are dependable individuals who will focus their efforts for your benefit if you treat them with the respect and consideration they deserve. By showing them you value their input, hard work, and flexibility, they will actively promote your big ideas to other people at networking events. Because Amiable Networkers place a high premium on loyalty and prefer to avoid confrontation, they will enthusiastically defend your ideas and goals when others may not be convinced of their merits.

COMMUNICATION WEAKNESSES OF AMIABLE NETWORKERS

If you are an Amiable Networker, your generally quiet manner can imply to other networkers that you are overly serious, hard to talk to, and uneasy in your surroundings. As a result, they may be more likely to gravitate to others who are more outgoing and whom they see as better candidates for business contacts. Here are some other conversational weaknesses associated with Amiable Networkers.

Shy or Passive in New Networking Situations

Some Amiable Networkers feel inhibited when they network in unfamiliar situations where they don't know anyone. Instead of using the time before a program to introduce themselves and meet new people, they take a seat away from the others and avoid eye contact by reading the agenda as they wait for the program to begin. Shy Amiable Networkers can attend networking events and not talk to anyone the whole time because they do not take the initiative to start conversations. As a result, shy Amiable

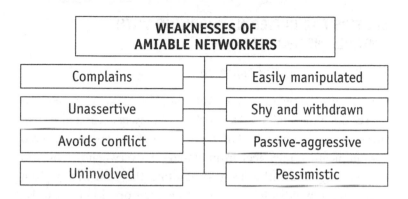

Networkers can give the false impression that they are disinterested and unwilling to connect.

Susceptible to Intimidation by More Talkative or Aggressive Networkers

Loud, overly talkative, or critical people can intimidate Amiable Networkers. As a result, Amiable Networkers may avoid conversations at networking events with these individuals, even if it means losing opportunities to make contact with potential prospects. As a result, if Amiable Networkers feel uncomfortable, they may try to leave conversations as quickly as possible.

Amiable Networkers Clam Up When Criticized

Most Amiable Networkers have high standards of achievement, yet if someone at a networking event criticizes their efforts or challenges their conclusions, they can become tongue-tied and angry. Instead of offering arguments and details to support their positions, they sink into deflated silence. Consequently, other networkers may view them as moody, lacking confidence, and unwilling to support a project in which they are involved.

SIX TIPS FOR BETTER NETWORKING WITH AMIABLE NETWORKERS

Tip #1: Use a Low-Key Approach

Competitive Networkers and Outgoing Networkers will get better results with Amiable Networkers if they use a toned-down, pressure-free approach. Otherwise, these somewhat reserved communicators may feel intimidated or overwhelmed by too much energy and enthusiasm. If you turn them off in your first encounter, it will be difficult to change their opinion of you. By talking more softly and slowly than you normally do, you will encourage Amiable Networkers to feel more comfortable in the opening minutes of your conversation.

Tip #2: Emphasize Teamwork and Collaboration

When you discuss business at networking events with Amiable Networkers, emphasize the role and value of teamwork. Describe how you and your colleagues have worked together on a recent project to overcome specific hurdles. Give examples to show your collaborative efforts. Give the credit to your team members and not to yourself or particular individuals.

Tip #3: Ask Open-Ended Questions

Ask Amiable Networkers to describe recent projects in which they have played a role. Your goal is to encourage them to open up and talk, so don't interrupt with examples of your own experiences, make sarcastic comments, or ask difficult questions— all of which may be interpreted as aggressive. Instead, carefully listen for implied statements, free information, and key words that suggest areas of mutual interest and other potential topics of conversation.

Tip #4: Explore the Emotions Behind Their Words and Actions

Amiable Networkers often imply their attitudes and feelings about issues and people rather than stating them directly. Instead of ignoring these hidden emotions and meanings or assuming that you fully understand them, ask Amiable Networkers to elaborate on implied statements if you sense that they want to talk more about particular subjecst. You will build a deeper sense of trust and rapport by showing interest in their feelings and opinions. However, do not push too hard for more information if they appear reluctant to elaborate.

Tip #5: Request Their Opinions and Help

One of the greatest compliments you can pay Amiable Networkers is to ask for their opinions or help. By asking for their opinions, you are saying that you value their knowledge, experience, and views. Your acknowledgment of their skills and abilities enhances their desire to help you. As a result, when you ask Amiable Networkers to introduce you to the right people, recommend a vendor, or provide a referral, they will be happy to comply.

Tip #6. Listen for Points of Agreement Without Interrupting

Show Amiable Networkers that you are listening and value their views by allowing them to complete their sentences without interruption. Never talk over Amiable Networkers with aggressive challenges, harsh criticism, or strongly worded opinions as this will only make them feel uncomfortable and want to withdraw from the conversation. Instead, smile and focus your responses on those points with which you agree.

AMIABLE NETWORKERS ARE LOYAL PARTNERS IN BIG DEALS

In this chapter you learned that Amiable Networkers are team players who don't mind letting others take the credit while they work behind the scenes. A little shy by nature, when you talk with Amiable Networkers, if you take a slightly low-key approach to networking with them, they will feel more comfortable opening up to you and discussing business. If you are an Amiable Networker, you now know that others will see you as more confident and outgoing if you actively engage people rather than wait for them to approach you. Once you show Amiable Networkers that you are a good listener and value their opinions, they can become among your most loyal professional contacts.

5

Breaking the Ice and Networking with Analytical Networkers

In this chapter you will learn:

- Characteristics and conversational traits of Analytical Networkers
- Communication strengths and weaknesses of Analytical Networkers
- Special tips to break the ice with Analytical Networkers
- How to adapt your conversations to Analytical Networkers

COMMUNICATION STRENGTHS OF ANALYTICAL NETWORKERS

If you are an Analytical Networker, you are a detailed-oriented person who prefers to communicate in a step-by-step manner based on facts and concrete concepts. People who like logic-based conversations like to network with you because your are articulate, knowledgeable, and willing to share your expertise.

Here are some additional communication strengths that are associated with Analytical Networkers.

Analytical Networkers Are Factual Listeners Who Value Accuracy and Logic

Analytical Networkers possess a high capacity for listening and assimilating large amounts of detailed information. They apply their logical approach of problem solving to networking. For example, by breaking down a complex business deal into its step-by-step components, they understand how it will work and where the project's shortcomings or failures may occur. As a result, based on facts and details presented to them, they make few mistakes or poor decisions. Analytical Networkers place a high premium on providing accurate information and correct answers.

Deliberate and Careful Speakers

Analytical Networkers style choose their words carefully. They are deliberate speakers who avoid making sweeping generalities, preferring to cite facts and figures that they can back up. How-

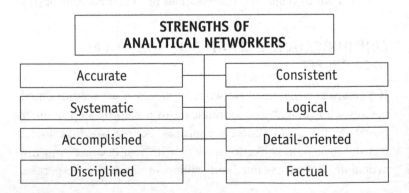

STRENGTHS OF ANALYTICAL NETWORKERS	
Accurate	Consistent
Systematic	Logical
Accomplished	Detail-oriented
Disciplined	Factual

ever, if you challenge Analytical Networkers, they can become competitive and will draw on their ability to present a logical and detailed case to support their views.

They Get Things Done Right

Analytical Networkers hate making mistakes! Consequently, they take their time to check and double-check that the information they have is correct so that any decisions or actions they take will result in the desired outcome. Their attention to detail, passion for problem solving, and ability to construct systematic solutions to achieve a specific goal makes them dependable and highly valued team members.

COMMUNICATION WEAKNESSES OF ANALYTICAL NETWORKERS

If you are an Analytical Networker, you tend to be passive, waiting for others to approach you, rather than being the first to initiate a conversation. In addition, you prefer to "talk shop" and may even have a strong dislike for small talk. When attending business and social events, you definitely feel more comfortable conversing one-on-one with peers versus meeting new people or joining other conversations already in progress. Here are some other conversational weaknesses associated with Analytical Networkers.

Focus Too Much on Detail and Overlook Implied Meanings

Analytical Networkers can focus so much on detail that they actually miss the implied statements, feelings, and true meanings behind the words they hear. Since they are motivated by accuracy, and not strictly by results, they can throw cold water on the ideas behind a big deal. When that happens, they do not see the big picture from the other person's perspective—that is, the overarching concepts, benefits, and objectives. As a result, Analytical Networkers have difficulty connecting with others who express themselves in broader and less structured ways at networking events.

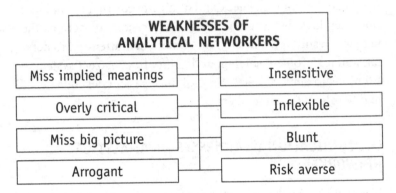

Listen Only for Flaws and What Can Go Wrong

Analytical Networkers can become fixated on talking about why an idea or a project will *not* work. In other words, they insist on hashing over minor points and dwelling on certain details that they see as inconsistent, illogical, or incorrect. By focusing and emphasizing only on what they see is wrong or flaws in an idea, Analytical Networkers inhibit the informal discussion and brainstorming that often takes place at networking events.

Analytical Networkers' overwhelming need to be right can create conflict with others who want to get the job done. Because of their strict orientation to order, their thinking can be rigid, and they can be stubborn. As a result, they can be unreceptive to alternative solutions or methods that fall outside their systematic approach.

A Tendency to Be Argumentative and a Know-It-All

"Are you sure about that?" What may seem like innocent questions or minor challenges about Analytical Networkers' facts or predictions can quickly provoke defensive and combative responses. A typical conversation at a networking event is instantly transformed into a loud battle of who is right and who is wrong with heated exchanges of facts, figures, challenges, and accusations for all to hear. When others conclude that Analytical Networkers are argumentative and "know-it-alls" they will probably choose to network with those they consider to be more open and receptive to new ideas.

SIX TIPS FOR BETTER NETWORKING WITH ANALYTICAL NETWORKERS

Tip #1: Allow Them to Play the Expert

Nothing will make Analytical Networkers like you more than giving them an opportunity to talk about what they know, offer their opinions, and share their experiences. By encouraging them to share their expertise and problem-solving abilities you are showing them that you value their ability and intelligence. This will set the stage for future conversations when you can take advantage of their analytical skills to help you identify and eliminate flaws in your big deals before you make formal proposals.

Tip #2: Avoid Small Talk Before Talking About More Serious Topics

Since many Analytical Networkers feel that small talk is a waste of time, it is wise to bring up more technical or business topics before chatting informally about other interests. Save any personal or light conversation for the end of your time together.

Tip #3: Be Accurate and Prepared

Because Analytical Networkers place a high value on accuracy, be sure that whatever information you give them is correct, up-to-date, and applicable, and that you can back it up
with facts and details. If you want to present some of the main
points of a big deal to someone with an analytical networking
style at an upcoming event, do the research to find the examples, facts, and credible sources that will back up your opinions
or projections.

Tip #4: Don't Gloss Over the Details

In discussing big deals at networking events with Analytical Networkers, offer plenty of details along with your big-picture
goals. If they ask, be ready to present the main steps from your
perspective, in order, from start to finish. The objective here is to
establish your credibility in their eyes so that they will take seriously your ideas and proposal for a big deal. If you only focus on
the big picture—that is, the benefits and goals—they may not
have enough facts to feel comfortable helping you with your
project.

Tip #5: Acknowledge Their Views

Since it is the nature of Analytical Networkers to focus on what
can go wrong, don't be surprised or get defensive when they
point out contradictions, mistakes, or false assumptions. People
with this style tend to see issues in terms of black and white,
right and wrong, and because of their strict orientation to order,
their thinking can be rigid. Rather than argue, you'll get better
results if you engage them in problem solving that leads to
achieving your goals.

Tip #6: Don't Debate—Find Areas of Agreement

On the surface, Analytical Networkers may appear to have passive natures. However, these individuals have a strong competitive streak and will vigorously argue over details, logic, or conclusions with which they disagree. Although you may think that a debate will lead to better communication, more often than not, the disagreement will leave one or both of you with bitter feelings about the exchange. Instead of highlighting differences, restrict your comments to areas of agreement.

ANALYTICAL NETWORKERS OFFER RELIABLE SOLUTIONS THAT LEAD TO BIG DEALS

In this chapter you learned that Analytical Networkers place a high emphasis on accuracy and logic. Now that you know some of their communication strengths and weaknesses, use their expertise, solid thinking, and attention to detail to help you achieve your big deals. If you are an Analytical Networker, you now understand that focusing on "what's right" as well as "what's wrong" will win you more business contacts. If you tap into the knowledge bases of Analytical Networkers, they will become among the most reliable information resources in your professional network.

PART II

CONNECTING ONLINE AND WORKING THE ROOM TO FIND BIG DEALS

6

Ten Strategic Networking Goals for Every Networking Event

In this chapter you will learn how to:

- **Define 10 strategic networking goals**
- **Uncover benefits in specific networking situations**
- **Link strategic networking goals to potential business**
- **Focus on long-term business goals**
- **Apply specific networking approaches to Networkers**

In my networking workshops, I ask the audience to come up with a list of ways they can benefit by attending business and social events. The first item on their list is nearly always "find new customers," but what other ways can you effectively use your time at networking events? Think about what you need to know, what you want to do, who you need to meet, and how you can find prospects that may lead to big deals.

People who attend events with some specific networking goals in mind—things they want to achieve during the time they spend meeting people and working the room—are more likely to achieve the key objectives necessary for their success. You can apply and adapt one or more of the following goals to many different networking situations. You may not always achieve every goal every time you network, but if you approach the process with some of these objectives in mind, you can't help but increase your number of contacts, referrals, and sales, not to mention appreciative colleagues.

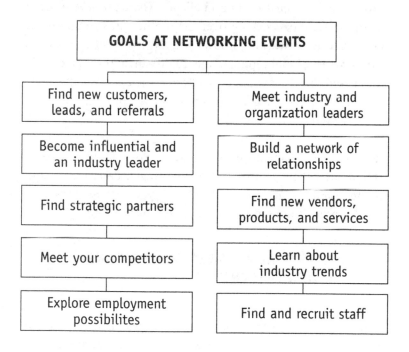

NETWORKING GOAL #1: FIND NEW CUSTOMERS, LEADS, AND REFERRALS

Most people say they attend networking events to find customers, get leads, and referrals. Why not? There are plenty of opportunities for finding and giving both. You establish yourself as a resource to and for others, plus, you are available when an opportunity for business presents itself.

Whether you are a business owner or a salesperson, you need to prospect for new customers because old customers retire or move on to other jobs, find better deals, or no longer need the products or services you offer. Most salespeople use a combination of cold calls, direct mail, advertising, and networking to prospect for new customers and clients. There are several benefits of strategic networking over these other prospecting methods. Strategic networking allows you to first meet face-to-face with prospects, build rapport, and qualify them through conversation, and then follow up with a "warm" telephone call or purposeful mail piece, such as a promised article or invitation to an industry event.

Reminder for Competitive Networkers. Your nature is to go straight after the big shots, but be sure to give *everyone* you talk to your *complete* attention. Do not let your gaze slip away to look for other "more important people" in the room.

NETWORKING GOAL #2: MEET INDUSTRY AND ORGANIZATION LEADERS

Meet the people who are the "movers and shakers" or centers of influence in the industries that you do business in and the organizations to which you belong or want to join. These are the people who have the best connections, know the most people, have the most experience, and can make the most powerful recommendations or referrals. Observe how these people network, conduct business, and interact. Then, using the four key networking styles, adapt their style to your way of doing business. Get to know these leaders and make an effort to find common interests and business goals. On occasion you can look to them for professional advice. If you don't overdo this, many are happy to share their knowledge and experience with you. Always reciprocate in some way, either directly to them or to the organization to which they belong.

Here are ways to meet industry or organization leaders:

- Arrive at events early so you can introduce yourself to the officers of the organization.
- Introduce yourself to presenters at organizations and events.
- Volunteer to help set up and take down chairs before and after events.
- E-mail organization leaders before the event saying that you hope to meet them at the event.
- Ask them how you can become more involved in their organizations.

Reminder for Outgoing Networkers. Your tendency to turn every conversation into a party can use up valuable networking time. Budget the length of your conversations based on how many people you want to meet in a given situation.

NETWORKING GOAL #3: BECOME INFLUENTIAL AND AN INDUSTRY LEADER

The next best thing to meeting a leader of an industry or organization is to become a leader or person of influence. As an industry leader, you will be looked at with high regard. Your opinions will be considered more valuable than your competitors'. As a networking strategy, being a leader puts you in an elevated position so that you can get both better pay and projects. When customers or clients have important jobs that require the best consultants, who do you think they call? They call the leaders in their industry, of course, because they are the people who are held in the highest esteem and who command the greatest respect.

Now you might think that this strategy is not for you, but you too can become a leader and a person of influence in your industry. Here are some ways to do that:

- Join industry organizations, get involved, and serve on member boards.
- Demonstrate leadership capabilities by taking on additional responsibilities.
- Present workshops at industry events in your area of expertise.
- Speak out on industry issues that affect your members and customers.
- Run or volunteer to be an officer of the organization.
- Write articles for your organizations' publications.

Reminder for Amiable Networkers. Your preference to be a "behind-the-scenes" player will limit your access to top industry and organization leaders. When you step up and volunteer to take a leadership role in your company or affiliated organizations, your professional image will grow and your proximity to people who can make big deals will increase.

NETWORKING GOAL #4: BUILD A NETWORK OF RELATIONSHIPS

When you attend a networking event, party, or even a family gathering, one of your goals can be to meet as many people from as many different professions as possible with the purpose of building a network of relationships. Your network is filled with people who are clients, customers, colleagues, friends, vendors, classmates, fraternity brothers, sorority sisters, parishioners, relatives, and many other people with whom you come in contact over your life on a regular basis.

The people who you bring into this network are those with opinions, ethics, values, credibility, capabilities, and sensibilities you trust and share. Trust is critical in the network of relationships because when you or someone in your network needs something or someone, everyone has to feel comfortable that the referral you either give or receive will be a good one.

While not all the people in your network will be your customers, those who are will think of you first when they or someone they know needs a person with your products or services. As you meet new prospects and colleagues, bring them into your network for your mutual benefit. Building a network of relationships can augment or even replace a strategy of cold calling to find prospects and new customers.

Reminder for Analytical Networkers. Your inclination is to focus your efforts on process, but don't forget that it is people who put together big deals.

NETWORKING GOAL #5: FIND STRATEGIC PARTNERS

In today's business world, it's impossible to do everything yourself. The good news is you don't need to! There are other people with whom you can partner who will help you. Finding those people is one of the goals of strategic networking. When you do, you can provide the products and services to your customers or clients that are outside your area of expertise or availability. Strategic partners allow you to pursue business opportunities outside your specific area of expertise to expand your services and products beyond your existing clients or customers.

This can enhance your professional image, because customers will see you as someone who has access to all the necessary elements to complete a big deal.

Granted, it's not easy to find the right strategic partners, but here are some tips people often forget:

- Look for people who have achieved an equal or higher level of success in their industry as you.
- Make sure their way of doing business is compatible with yours.
- Clarify expectations and responsibilities.
- Make your business arrangements simple, clear, and legal, and put them in writing.

Reminder for Competitive Networkers. "I call the shots!" is the mantra of many Competitive Networkers, but if you need a partner to seal a big deal, you'll need to share the power as well as the glory.

NETWORKING GOAL #6: FIND NEW VENDORS, PRODUCTS, AND SERVICES

There are several benefits to meeting vendors at networking events, particularly those that are industry related. First, it gives you an opportunity to compare prices and learn about new products and services. If you're not happy with your current suppliers, meeting vendors provides the possibility of finding new suppliers who are more reliable, economical, or to your liking. Finding and qualifying other available vendors gives you a backup for existing suppliers, just in case they have an emergency or, even worse, go out of business. Plus, it is a way to augment your existing suppliers if they are not capable of handling larger orders. To qualify a vendor you can ask:

- "Who have you worked with in this organization or industry that I might know?"
- "How does your company's . . . program differ from Company ABC's program?"
- "What software do you recommend for . . . ?"
- "I'm not entirely happy with . . . . Does your company offer one that I might like better?"

Reminder for Outgoing Networkers. Your desire to please others may make you feel obligated to refer new contact to your friends, vendors, or clients. However, before you put their credibility and your reputation on the line, make sure they can deliver on their promises. The best policy is to recommend people and businesses with whom you have direct personal experience or whose recommendation comes from a reliable source.

NETWORKING GOAL #7: MEET YOUR COMPETITORS

Every so often I am invited to a fancy dinner at one of New York's best restaurants to join a publisher, other authors, editors, entrepreneurs, doctors, attorneys, politicians, and other businesspeople to meet, share great food, and enjoy stimulating conversation. For one dinner in particular, I was thrilled when I saw the name of one of my competitors on the guest list. I'd read her books, and we even belonged to the same professional speakers association, but we'd never met. We sat next to each other and shared plenty of news and views about publishing, training, and where our services and products overlapped and how they were different. We were what you could describe as "friendly competitors." Having a friendly competitor relationship can pay off. Although you and your friendly competitors may go after the same business, you can also do joint ventures, discuss common problems, or refer overflow business to one another.

Of course, not all the competitors you meet at networking events will be friendly or open. In that case, quietly observe how they do the following:

- Attract prospects
- Describe their customer service
- Pitch their products and services
- Position themselves in the market

What do you see as your competitors' strengths and weaknesses? Where is your competitive edge? This valuable "competitive intelligence" can help you set yourself apart from your competition when you are pitching your products, services, and big deals.

Reminder for Amiable Networkers. Since your nature is to avoid confrontation whenever possible, you might shy away from talking to your competitors. However, consider these conversations opportunities to connect and position yourself as a resource. With so many people frequently changing positions, and with companies dropping products or services, you never know when a competitor might turn into a customer.

NETWORKING GOAL #8: LEARN ABOUT INDUSTRY TRENDS

Learn as much as you can about your industry. Here are just a couple of the questions that you can find answers to at networking events:

- Where does your company, product, or service fit in?
- What are the changes taking place, and are you keeping up with them?

- What are the trends in your industry, and are you preparing to take advantage of them?
- Are your products, services, staff, and strategies ready to meet these challenges?
- What changes will you need to make if you are to remain competitive?
- What short, medium, and long-term decisions do you need to make *now* based on where your industry is going?

Reminder for Analytical Networkers. Your quick and logical mind certainly can assess the application of new products for the market. Remember, however, if you are overly critical of someone's project or product, it will only make you look argumentative or petty.

NETWORKING GOAL #9: EXPLORE EMPLOYMENT POSSIBILITIES

If you're on the lookout for a new position with a high salary, lots of incentives, upward mobility, and great benefits, don't just look in the newspapers, because you probably won't find it there. Instead, go to networking events in the industry that you want to work in. There you will find people who know people in the companies that you want to work for. Using small talk and other networking skills, you can find out who works for whom and if there are any openings.

Depending on the event, you might even meet the people who are in a position to get you an interview, recommend you, or even hire you. Also, depending on who you talk to, you can get the lowdown on companies, supervisors, projects, and other information that can help you determine if this is an employer that you would like to work for.

At networking events not everyone is open to discussing employment status or plans for job changes. However, it's not uncommon to find sales representatives working the floors at trade shows, conventions, and other industry functions who will chat openly about this topic. Therefore, here are a few examples of how to casually open a conversation about employment opportunities with someone at a networking event. First get an idea of how the person feels about his or her job and employer with questions such as:

- "What's it like working for your company?"
- "How long have you been with the company? Do you like it?"
- "Are you planning on staying, or are you looking around?"

If the reaction is generally positive and you want to pursue the topic further, then you can say something like:

- "I've always got my eyes open for new employment possibilities. What's the job situation in your department?"
- "I've heard good things about your company, and I'd love to see about getting a job there. Do you have any suggestions on how I might do that, or do you know someone I could talk to?"

Reminder for All Networkers. Be cautious about revealing your desire to change jobs when sniffing around for other employment possibilities. If someone asks you, "Are you looking for a new job?" you can say, "I have a friend who may consider a move if the right opportunity comes up."

NETWORKING GOAL #10: FIND AND RECRUIT STAFF

If you're looking for qualified people to fill open positions in your department or company, you can put an ad in the newspaper, go through an employment service, or list the position on any of the many job Web sites. Of course, with an employment service, you have to pay a fee, and with ads in the newspapers and on Web sites you get many candidates, however most will be unqualified. Both of these ways of recruiting are time-consuming and expensive. Networking offers another alternative and can be part of your staffing strategy.

Smart and experienced job seekers know that their best chance of finding a good position is through networking at industry-related events. Therefore, it makes sense that employers can find many qualified applicants in the same situation. The goal is to bring together the job seeker with the job provider. Here's how you can spread the word that you are looking for a qualified applicant for an open position:

- "If you meet anyone here tonight who is experienced in . . . and is looking to change positions, please introduce that person to me."
- "Since we're on the subject of finding good people, I'm on the lookout for someone to fill a very special position. If you know anyone with experience who is interested in . . . , have the person give me call. Here's my card."

Reminder for All Networkers. Employee raiding, or "poaching"—that is, the practice of wooing an employee to leave one employer for another to gain inside information or special skills—may be tempting, but it can cause ethical and legal problems. Plus, it will almost certainly result in a breach of trust between you and your colleagues in your industry.

LINKING STRATEGIC NETWORKING GOALS
TO YOUR BUSINESS GOALS

You may not always achieve every one of the goals presented here each time you attend a networking event. However, if you approach the process with some of these objectives in mind and they are linked directly to your business goals, you can't help but increase your number of contacts, referrals, and sales, not to mention friends and appreciative colleagues.

7

Four Ways to Use a Guest List to Increase Networking Results

In this chapter you will learn how to use a guest list to:

- Manage your time at networking events
- Prioritize prospects at events
- Help you remember names
- Conduct online research about prospects and companies
- Know what to talk about to particular individuals
- Sound informative and demonstrate industry knowledge

Do you remember the last time you walked into a roomful of people at a business or social event and wondered, "Who are all these people and do I know anyone here?" Instead of entering networking functions and looking like a deer in the headlights, there is an easy and highly effective networking technique you can do beforehand to help you quickly connect with others.

REQUEST A GUEST LIST *BEFORE* THE EVENT

If there is one thing I've learned that can make a difference
between meeting productive contacts and missing golden opportunities at a networking event, it's getting a copy of the guest or
attendee list. Although some organizations have strict rules
against giving out their lists unless you are a paid vendor attending the event, others are more relaxed about it. In many cases if
you just ask for it, they will e-mail or fax you their lists. However,
sometimes you need to offer your reasons and an assurance that
you will not use the lists for marketing purposes.

For example, when one event organizer told me that her
organization sends out the list of attendees *after* the event, I
explained to her that having the list beforehand helps me and
others to network, which is one of the reasons we attend events
in the first place. I also promised not to use the list for marketing
or to pass it on to anyone else. She then happily e-mailed me the
list of about 25 people. I was grateful because I saw the names of
several potential clients with whom I wanted to speak and the
better prepared I was for our conversations, the more likely our
chats were to bear fruit. Once you receive a guest list, you can
use it in at least four ways to increase the effectiveness of your
networking.

1. Prioritize and Target Prospects That You Want to Contact

Since you probably will not be able to meet or talk to everyone
at the event, having the guest list ahead of time gives you the
opportunity to look it over and prioritize the people with
whom you want to make contact—for their benefit and for
yours. Usually there are four categories of people you will see
on the guest list:

- *High-potential prospects.* First, there are the high-potential prospects that you really want to meet. Plan to spend most of your time meeting and talking with these people, as they are the ones who are most likely to lead you to the big deals.
- *Prior acquaintances.* Second, you will likely see some people on the list whom you've met before. Plan on spending at least several minutes to reconnect with each of them and, hopefully, move your relationship to the next level.
- *Friends and colleagues.* Third, you will probably see some friends, colleagues, competitors, and vendors. Set aside a few minutes to say hello to them too, and if time permits, have a brief chat.
- *Strangers.* Finally, there are those people who you know nothing about, yet who may be valuable networking contacts. Here is where some quick online research can open many potential business conversations. Also, you can call or e-mail your colleagues on the guest list and ask them if they know anything about the people you have not met. You might find an interesting connection or opportunity.

Reminder for All Networkers. While you want to focus the majority of your networking efforts on high-potential prospects, don't overlook the long-term benefits of introducing yourself to new people and expanding existing business relationships.

2. Get a Head Start on Remembering People's Names

You can use the guest list to do what most people admit they fail miserably at—remembering names. Here are some easy ways to use the guest list to help you remember the names of the people you meet:

- First, review the names aloud, one by one. To remember familiar names, think of someone you know with the same name—a friend, a spouse, an old classmate, or even a celebrity—and when you meet that person at the event, associate him or her with the other person.
- Next, take note of how many people on the guest list share first names. The likely high number of people with the same names will surprise you. As you meet these people at the event, visually connecting them will help you remember all their names.
- Take a few extra moments to review and say aloud the unfamiliar names on the guest list. Spelling the name and making a mental note of words that rhyme with it or sound similar to it will help you remember the name when you meet the person.
- Finally, the day or evening of the event, slip the guest list into your coat jacket or pocket so you can discreetly refer to it if you cannot recall another guest's name.

Taking a few minutes to review the guest list pays off. You will make a big impression if you remember the names of the people at the events, and the guest list will help you learn them in advance. Finally, you will make people feel good about you and themselves when you say, "I saw your name on the guest list, and I wanted to be sure to meet you."

3. Do Online Research on Target Prospects, Key Executives and Companies, and Industry News

Another valuable use of the guest list is to do targeted research on the Internet about the people attending the networking event and their companies —including your competition. Let's say you see the name of a company's key executive on the guest list for an event and you think that he or she may be a high potential prospect. With just a few mouse clicks and within a few minutes or so, you can find out about these things:

- The company history
- The company's mission statement
- Executives and their roles in the organization
- Recent company news and promotions
- Current projects and needs
- Your target prospect's job description and past experience

Reminder for All Networkers. Although knowing people's profession and position can give you hints to their particular networking styles, be ready to immediately adapt your conversation to better fit with their actual ways of communicating.

- *Use online research for relevant topics to break the ice.* Here are some ways to use online research to facilitate your conversations and improve your networking results. You can break the ice and then slant your conversations toward issues that are relevant to the organization and the individual. Topics and people referred to on the company's Web site or blogs are the best ones to use to start conversations at networking events. Also have a wide range of general-interest topics related to their business at your fingertips. This will facilitate relaxed and informal conversation for those prospects who prefer making small talk before discussing business. These related topics give you an opportunity to naturally segue to business topics.

- *Use online research to demonstrate your industry awareness.* Knowing news about a company or an individual demonstrates that you pay attention to what is happening in their industry. Usually, prospects are flattered if you mention that you read a blog, a media story, or an online article about them or their company. Consider ahead of time open-ended questions that will allow you to guide the conversation to areas where you may have the opportunity to naturally reveal your area of expertise.

   Industry-related topics that focus on technology, sales, and business initiatives are a good way to break the protective wall that surrounds many Competitive and Analytical Networkers. Industry topics related to training, human resources, and teams are excellent ice-breakers with most Outgoing and Amiable Networkers.

- *Use online research to demonstrate your knowledge of your competition.* If you know which of your competitors are attending an event, you can go to their Web sites and study their products or services so that you can intelligently compare and discuss them with prospects and colleagues. Also, knowing if your competitors are attending an event tells you if they also see potential for business in that market.

- *Use online research to link your areas of expertise to the current needs of individuals and organizations.* Knowing the current needs and goals of an individual or the organization before you attend the event helps you identify and express specific capabilities you can offer. It also gives you an opportunity to reach into your network of associates to be ready to offer them as a resource to the person or company.

4. Send Targeted Prospects an Invitation to Meet

You can consider sending certain individuals on the guest list a brief and friendly (not hard selling or marketing) e-mail or note saying that you also will be at the event and that you would like an opportunity to meet. Showing a desire to connect demonstrates that you are friendly, confident, and goal oriented, plus it allows the prospect to prepare for a conversation with you. In addition, a short, well-written e-mail eliminates a "cold" introduction at the event and some of the discomfort that often exists between strangers when they meet for the first time. I strongly urge you to proofread your e-mails at least a couple of times for spelling, grammar, and clarity before clicking the send button. Remember, first impressions count—even in e-mails—so make them error-free and professional.

Reminder for Competitive Networkers. Skip hard sell invitations for more informal requests to meet.

Reminder for Outgoing Networkers. Make your invitations brief, neatly written, and focused on a specific topic or outcome.

Reminder for Amiable Networkers. Take the initiative to send invitations rather than waiting for others to reach out to you first.

Reminder for Analytical Networkers. Keep your invitations light and friendly.

A QUICK LOOK AT A GUEST LIST WILL PAY OFF BIG!

Doing online research based on the guest list before an event demonstrates that you have specific goals to achieve when you network. It shows that you are a person who organizes your time for an intended result and a person who uses a systematic approach to uncovering business opportunities. Most prospects consider these valuable qualities. With as little as an hour of research and prep time, your confidence and focus will soar the next time you network at a business or social event. When that happens, you increase your chances of finding productive leads and contacts—and that's what strategic networking is all about!

Five Steps to Joining
Other Conversations

In this chapter you will learn how to:

- Identify receptive groups at networking events
- Approach groups and know what to say
- Quickly join conversations already in progress
- Be accepted into the conversation

Any successful networker will tell you that if you want to get real results from attending business or social events, you need to meet and talk to as many "qualified" people as possible. While there are many times when you want to network one-on-one, you'll increase your odds of making contact with people who can lead you to a big deal if you join conversations currently in progress.

However, some people are reluctant to join others already engaged in conversation. These people often say that they feel uncomfortable doing this because they think the people talking already know each other. They also probably think that the people talking prefer the company of their friends and will not be interested in what outsiders have to say. In most cases, these are false assumptions, and the sooner you correct them, the sooner you'll feel more confident joining ongoing conversations. Here are five steps to help you become a part of conversations already in progress.

FIVE STEPS TO JOINING OTHER CONVERSATIONS ALREADY IN PROGRESS

As soon as you enter the room, look around to see how people are situated and who is talking to whom. Most people talking to one another will be standing or sitting in pairs and clusters of three, four, or maybe even more. Some of the people in the groups will be members, and some will be newcomers like you. Some will be animated and talkative, while others will be reserved and quiet. No matter what their conversation styles are, if you approach the group the right way, you'll be welcome.

Step 1: Look for Open Groups—Avoid Closed Groups

Your first step is to identify open and closed groups, first from a body language perspective and then from a content perspective. An open group consists of people standing or sitting in such a way as to leave enough space between them so that an outsider can easily join their conversation. Their individual body language includes smiling, unfolded arms, and plenty of eye contact. On the other hand, a closed group consists of people who may be standing or situated so close together that there is little room for an outsider to join them. Their individual body language reveals little smiling, shifting eyes, little eye contact, crossed arms, and covered mouths or chins using one or both hands.

Generally speaking, if you see that most of the people chatting in a group have closed body language, look for another group to join. If you spot a targeted prospect in that group, wait for what appears to be a better time to approach the person. However, if it's late in the event, this may be your last chance to make contact, so move closer to the group.

Reminder for Amiable and Analytical Networkers. Instead of hanging out with your buddies in the corner, circulate through the room. Keep your body language friendly as you search for groups displaying an openness to others.

Step 2: Move Within "Eavesdropping" Distance

You need to be within three to five feet of the group to overhear their conversation. Are you eavesdropping? The answer is yes, but how else can you assess whether you want to join the conversation or move on to another group? Based on what you hear and see, avoid approaching the group if:

- Their conversation is deadly serious or stilted
- The people are grousing about a boss or gossiping about a client
- One person is doing most of the talking while others silently stand by
- Two people are having a heated discussion over politics or other controversial topics
- You see others in the group glancing at each other and appearing uncomfortable
- Several people have excused themselves from the group

Based on what you see and hear, get ready to join a group if:

- The conversation sounds animated and upbeat
- Most of the people are participating and sound like they are enjoying themselves
- Their discussion is most likely centered around the networking event, business, sports, food, travel, or other high-interest positive topics that most people can participate in
- They are also chatting between themselves within the group, exchanging names and shaking hands
- Within just a few minutes, you can see the group increase in size with added newcomers

Reminder for All Networkers. "Lurk" and listen in for a minute or so to assess the group's openness and your level of interest in the topic under discussion. Then either approach the group or move on.

Step 3: Establish Eye Contact and Smile at the People in the Group

Assuming that you want to join a particular conversation, move still closer toward the group and look for an open space between two of the participants. Establish eye contact with and smile at each person in the group as he or she speaks. Also establish eye contact and smile at other people who are in the group who are listening. Nod your head to acknowledge that you agree with something that you've just heard. These nonverbal signals—eye contact, smiling, nodding, and moving closer—are sending a clear message that you find a conversation interesting and that you want to join the group. Keep listening and look for someone in the group who smiles back and establishes eye contact with you. Consider this a nonverbal invitation to approach the group and then get ready to break the ice.

Reminder for Analytical Networkers. When someone from a group makes eye contact with you and smiles, do not avoid the gaze. Immediately make eye contact, slightly nod your head, smile back to acknowledge the greeting, and approach the group.

Step 4: Ask an Easy-to-Answer Question or Make a Positive Comment

Now you must pay close attention to timing, because to interrupt someone in the middle of a statement would probably be considered rude or might offend someone in the group. Follow the conversation as if you are already part of the group as a listener, but not yet as a participant. Nod your head again to show that you are listening. Smile as the speakers make their points to acknowledge that you approve of what they are saying.

When there is a brief pause in the conversation, that's the time for you to speak up and ask an easy-to-answer question or share a positive comment. Never contradict any of the speakers, since that would make it sound as if you were looking for an argument or wanted to make yourself look good at someone else's expense. You can address one or all of the speakers. The objective is to interact in a nonthreatening way that clearly demonstrates that you want to join the conversation. As soon as someone answers your question or responds to your comments, move directly into the available space in the group. If you want to be absolutely sure that you are welcome to join the group, you can ask, "Do you mind if I join you?"

Reminder for Competitive Networkers and Analytical Networkers. Attempting to join the conversation by challenging something someone said in the group will probably come across as crass, aggressive, or argumentative. Be sure to keep your questions easy, and your comments positive; don't contradict or call into question anything said. Your goal is to join the group, not to get into a debate.

Step 5: Introduce Yourself and Ask an Open-Ended Follow-Up Question

After a brief moment, introduce yourself to the people in the group. Be sure to give each person your full attention and take your time as you shake hands and repeat names aloud. Then pick up the conversation right where you left off by asking an open-ended question based on what you've already heard. "I'd like to hear more about . . ." is a safe way to get the others talking again and give you an opportunity to get a feel for the conversation before plunging in head first. Participate in the conversation as you would in any other, because now you are part of the group. As you talk and listen, position yourself in the group in such a way as to leave some additional space for anyone else who may want to join your conversation.

Reminder for Outgoing Networkers. Take care to tone down the volume of your voice. Do not try to impress others or take over the conversation by talking too much, especially if the group is made up of more reserved Amiable Networkers or Analytical Networkers.

JOINING GROUP CONVERSATIONS IS EASY AND WILL INCREASE YOUR NUMBER OF POTENTIAL BUSINESS CONTACTS

One of the big advantages of networking in groups is that it allows you to quickly spread the word about who you are and what you do to more people than by having only one-on-one conversations. At the same time, group conversations allow you to find out about the experiences and needs of many others. In the end, networking can be looked at as a numbers game where the player with the most useful contacts wins!

9

Making Business Connections on Social Networks

In this chapter you will learn how to:

- **Get started networking on social networking sites**
- **Create a professional online networking profile**
- **Extend invitations on social networks**
- **Exercise correct social network etiquette**
- **Build credibility and expand your social network contacts**

As someone who places a high value on face-to-face relationships, I admit that I was skeptical of all the hoopla surrounding social networks like MySpace and Facebook. I considered these Web sites as nothing more than virtual malls for kids stuck at home who wanted to hang out with their friends. I was concerned (and still am to a certain degree) that young people who spend more time e-mailing and text messaging their "friends" than talking to them in person are at risk of losing—or never even learning—the critical interpersonal communication skills necessary for them to succeed in their professional, social, and personal lives.

However, I've changed my opinion about their value for business and career development, and now I feel that there are many reasons for you to incorporate social networking into your traditional networking activities. First, today professionals from practically every industry have specialized social networks where they regularly exchange views, discuss trends, make recommendations, and present employment opportunities. In fact, according to a recent survey published by the National Association of Colleges and Employers, more than half of the employers questioned will use social networking sites to connect with potential candidates. Of course, whether you make small talk with people in person or on a social networking site, your ability to accurately determine another's networking style will greatly enhance your communication, quickly facilitate rapport, and lead you closer to making a big deal.

GET STARTED BY SIGNING UP FOR AN ACCOUNT WITH LINKEDIN, FACEBOOK, OR MYSPACE

One of the people who helped change my mind was Lee Aase, chancellor of Social Media University, Global (SMUG), a higher education institution for lifelong learners who want to discuss how to effectively incorporate social media into their work. In his blog, Aase wrote, "Part of my job at Mayo Clinic is about understanding new media and social media and their possible business uses. I finally needed to see [Facebook] for myself, and signed up for an account." He goes on to say, "I believe Facebook will transform networking on the web from a largely social, recreational activity to one that has serious implications for business."

While Lee Aase gives a nod to LinkedIn and other professional-oriented sites, clearly, Facebook is his favorite. He points out, "Facebook has 30 million users, so if you want to connect with the general public, not just people in your own profession, you can use Facebook to reach networks of networks. You can't count out MySpace, with its more than 100 million users, but clearly Facebook has the momentum and is creating a win-win-win environment for its users, for partner businesses, and for itself."

Whatever social networks you prefer to frequent, they are great places to meet people and network and, no matter what your personal networking style, media gurus agree that social networks offer a potent and efficient way for you to connect with your market and customers. Here are some tips from social networking pros to help you more effectively enter into and benefit from this brave new marketplace.

1. Create a Well-Written Profile That Establishes Your Credibility

All online business experts agree that your credibility starts with your profile. "Make sure your profile represents you the way you want to be viewed by strangers," suggests Liz Ryan, online entrepreneur and author of *Happy About Online Networking*. "An incomplete profile, for example, won't serve you as you network on LinkedIn." Ryan advises networkers to "fill in the gaps" or they will send a message that all they want from the social network is to use the database to find people, but won't bother to include enough information about themselves to indicate how they might help others. A tip from the LinkedIn Blogspot suggests using key words in your profile so that your profile pops up when others search it.

On another profile issue, business writing experts and authors Marilynne Rudick and Leslie O'Flahavan of E-WRITE, a training and consulting company that specializes in writing for online readers, emphasize, "Online readers expect a personal, upbeat tone in web writing. They find bureaucratic writing offensive and out-of-place." They also stress avoiding jargon and carefully proofreading your writing before posting.

2. Practice "Invitation Etiquette" as You Reach Out to Other Members

Tim O'Reilly, publisher of the technology news Web site O'Reilly Radar, cautions against sending complete strangers online boiler-plate invitations such as "I'd like to add you to my professional network on LinkedIn" because he, for one, puts them right into the trash. He adds, "If I've met you, I might need my mind jogged."

To increase the likelihood of having your online invitation accepted, experts suggest you be polite, brief, direct, and person-alize your invitation with: 1) the person's name spelled correctly, 2) if you've met, say when and where; 3) a few words about your-self; 4) why you are making contact, and 5) a specific request such as "Please add me as a contact" or "May I ask you a few questions about . . . ?"

Is sending an invitation to someone who rejects your request a mistake? LinkedIn user Matthew Ringman, regional purchasing manager at SCP Distributors, LLC, put it this way, "I wouldn't call sending out an invitation and not getting a response back a mistake. If someone doesn't want to connect, it's not a big deal."

3. Manage the Number of Your Online Contacts

Social media strategist Howard Greenstein leads the Harbrooke Group and helps firms understand and adopt the technologies and practices that allow them to better communicate with their customers. When it comes to making friends on social networking sites, Greenstein councils, "While it looks good in your LinkedIn profile that you have 500+ friends, it's a challenge to manage that number of relationships. Keep your online contacts limited to those with whom you can maintain meaningful contact."

Monte Enbysk, a senior editor at Microsoft Office Live and writer who specializes in Web-related issues for small businesses, says that experts make great business contacts. He suggests, "Seek out recognized authorities in your field." In his online column, Office Hours, he also says that having a small number of friends (or connections) who value your passions and expertise, and who care to network regularly, may be best for your business."

4. Meet Social Networking Contacts Face-to-Face or Talk on the Telephone

Greenstein emphasizes, "Social networking tools do not replace the need for people to meet in person." Other social media experts agree that when it comes to business contacts, e-mail, instant messaging, blogs, and other online contact software are great stepping-off points. But in face-to-face contact, you have the opportunity to build the necessary rapport that is more likely to cement the relationship. Consider joining a Meetup Group in your area on your topic or field of expertise and move your virtual relationships into the real world. If meeting in person is not practical, then pick up the telephone and give your online contact a call to say hello.

5. Ask Questions, Offer Answers, and Request and Write Recommendations

Kay Luo, director of Corporate Communications at LinkedIn, suggests that LinkedIn members try Answers—a new service that lets users post and answer questions. Luo says, "By taking the time to provide thoughtful information, you will build your credibility in the system. The better your response, the more people will want to look at your profile. This will help you to build your social capital with your own network."

When you ask for an endorsement from a contact, instead of just sending LinkedIn's boilerplate, "I'm sending this to ask you for a brief recommendation of my work that I can include in my LinkedIn profile. If you have any questions, let me know. Thanks in advance for helping me out," personalize your request with something like this: "I'd appreciate your telling other members how I helped you and your company to . . . ."

LinkedIn can also help you build your online credibility and professional profile. Its Answers feature encourages members to ask one another questions and to exchange their professional expertise. By posting answers, members earn expertise points in particular categories. The higher number of points a member earns, the higher his or her name appears on the list of experts. For example, Matthew Ringman, a specialist in purchasing and forecasting multimillion dollar inventories, warehouse management software, and inventory control over multibranch region, spends most of his time on LinkedIn using the questions and answers forums. "I see this feature as a great resource for people who are still trying to understand how things work by asking, 'Hey, how do I do this?'"

Concerning recommendations, Greenstein suggests a cautious approach. "How well do you know the person you are recommending? Can you personally vouch for his or her abilities, ethics, and experience? If not, then consider a pass, because all it takes is one bad recommendation from you to ruin your online reputation."

6. Stay in Touch and Follow Your Contacts' Career Paths

Herb Hogue is a principal business consultant for Agilysys, Inc., a leading provider of innovative IT solutions serving corporate and public-sector customers. He says LinkedIn assisted him in opening a network of people he needed to contact for a specific function and helps him stay in contact with people he has met throughout his career. "I'm in the IT arena, and people move around a lot. It's interesting because it gives you their career path and lets you see where they are. We all have business contacts that we don't necessarily keep close ties with. LinkedIn allows you to stay in contact."

7. Avoid Aggressive Marketing to Your Social Network of Contacts

Media consultants generally agree that overly aggressive marketing on social networks is counterproductive. Instead they suggest that marketers provide something of value to members by personalizing their contacts and regularly updating their content. When it comes to aggressive marketing and constant promotion on social networking sites, Monte Enbysk warns, "If you do nothing but promote your new book or new business or product, people in your network will lose interest and likely 'un-friend' you." Lee Aase agrees, "Doing an announcement can generate excitement, but repeating your news again and again is frowned upon. It's better to create interesting content that relates to the new book or business that earns the reader's attention."

Sending useful content and maintaining meaningful contact through social networks requires tact as well as sensitivity to your audience. Leslie O'Flahavan, an authority on writing e-mails and online communication, cautions people to consider the kind of content they send others. "Every time I want to communicate with people in my network I have to wonder if they are going to welcome this kind of communication." She goes on to say that some decisions are easy. Examples include offering a resource to her network or letting them know about a conference at which she is speaking. "But if I'm offering a course where I'm charging tuition, I'm not at all sure it's okay to let them know," she admits. "There's no rule anywhere on LinkedIn. I have contacts who I respect who are marketing to me. It's a decision I have to make on my own. And like all social networks, you learn how they work by observing them and deciding who in the network you want to be like and who you want to be different from."

8. Keep Up on the Buzz About Web 2.0

"It's the hottest topic all over the blogs!" Let's face it, if you don't know what people are talking about in the blogosphere or on industry-related social networking sites, then you are simply behind the curve—and your competitors! Web 2.0 technologies and trends sprout up every day, so it's wise to pay attention to what's happening in the fast-changing world of social networking. Lee LeFever, principal of Common Craft, produces short online videos that make learning about Web 2.0 fast, fun, and easy. Common Craft presents social networking products and services in "Plain English," using short, unique, and understandable video format called "Paperworks."

Also, check out Technorati, the recognized authority on what's happening on the World Live Web right now. It currently tracks 112.8 million blogs and over 250 million pieces of tagged social media, and it claims that, "there are 175,000 new blogs every day. Bloggers update their blogs regularly to the tune of over 1.6 million posts per day, or over 18 updates a second." In one of his excellent programs, "RSS in Plain English," LeFever suggests that to effectively access the online information that most interests you, subscribe to RSS (Really Simple Syndication) feeds so that you automatically get updated blogs and bulletins.

9. Let Others Get to Know You as a Social Network Member, Not as a Marketer

Social media experts suggest that after exploring a number of social networking sites, people should actively participate in a few. Engage in online discussion forums, answer questions, and write comments on blogs. Introduce yourself and offer referrals when appropriate. By letting others get to know you as a member, not as a marketer, you will achieve the promise of social networking: connecting with an online community of people who share your interests and activities.

BUILDING RELATIONSHIPS ON SOCIAL NETWORKS CREATES REAL-WORLD OPPORTUNITIES

Now that you know more about how to connect and network using LinkedIn and other social networking sites, you have an opportunity to build relationships with others who share your interests, needs, goals, and experiences. Through small talk and networking, you will send the message that others, as well as yourself, can benefit from this relationship as business opportunities arise.

10

Six Steps to Turn Small Talk into Big-Deal Discussions

In this chapter you will learn how to:

- Guide your conversations to business topics with small talk
- Use small talk to build rapport and credibility and uncover prospects' needs
- Improve your timing when bringing up business topics
- Link your capabilities with the other person's needs
- Ask for a follow-up appointment

WHY IS SMALL TALK SO IMPORTANT TO BUSINESS CONVERSATIONS?

In the previous chapters you've learned about four networking styles, many networking strategies, ways to join conversations in progress, and how to make contacts through online social networks. However, for these networking opportunities to bear fruit, you'll need to use your communication skills to direct the conversations to more specific business issues—and that's where small talk plays such an important role. Now I know that for some businesspeople, small talk at networking events seems like nothing more than frivolous chitchat and a waste of time. However, nothing could be further from the truth. Small talk is the fastest and easiest way to connect with strangers, find out their status or position, and build rapport, trust, and much more. Small talk allows networkers to quickly and informally:

- Create a picture of who they are, their background, experience, and expertise
- Find common business interests, goals, needs, and values
- Establish credibility and likability
- Determine and adapt to different networking styles

When and how you change the topic from small talk to a big-deal discussion varies depending on if you are networking in a business, social, or public situation. If you are at a business-related networking event, it's generally acceptable to bring up a business topic soon after you've met. However, in social or public situations it is best to wait until you hear a keyword or phrase that suggests a willingness to discuss a business topic. Follow these steps for making a smooth move from small talk to a business conversation.

Step 1: Immediately Engage, Interact, and Listen

In most cases, if you make small talk right away, you'll soon break down the barriers that separate strangers, plus you'll be the one in the best position to guide the conversation. Don't think about what you are going to say next—instead engage, interact, and listen for words that suggest business topics. Also take note

---

SIX STEPS TO TRANSITION FROM SMALL TALK TO A BIG-DEAL DISCUSSION

Step 1: Immediately Engage, Interact, and Listen
Step 2: Zero In on Business-Related Keywords
Step 3: Refer to a Business-Related Keyword or Phrase
Step 4: Move the Conversation to Bigger Business Issues
Step 5: Link Your Capabilities to the Prospect's Needs
Step 6: If You Get a "Buy Signal," Ask for an Appointment

---

of body language, tone of voice, and overall response. This will help you assess your conversation partner's networking style and make the necessary adjustments. Your goal is to make the other person feel comfortable talking to you as quickly as possible.

Reminder for Competitive Networkers. Show you know how to listen. Avoid instant assessments or smug pronouncements. Ask others for more information and their opinions.

Reminder for Outgoing Networkers. Listen without interrupting. Make an extra effort to let others complete their sentences before offering your opinions or ideas.

Reminder for Amiable Networkers. Contribute more to the conversation by actively interjecting your ideas and opinions into the dialogue. Show a deeper interest with follow-up questions and relevant experiences that focus on the specific business issues of others.

Reminder for Analytical Networkers. Pay special attention to your body language: smile and have consistent eye contact and don't roll your eyes. Also keep the tone of your voice friendly and don't criticize, pronounce judgments, or offer complicated solutions. Instead, encourage others to elaborate on their most important issues and desired outcomes.

Step 2: Zero In on Business-Related Keywords

Making the transition from small talk to a business discussion is easy if you listen for and refer to keywords that fall into these six categories: *people, places, things, activities, situations,* and especially, *challenges.* When someone you are talking to mentions one or more of the following keywords, that is your cue to use that word to follow up and ask more information so you can change the subject to business. Here are just a few of the many examples of keywords that fall into these categories:

PEOPLE
- Clients
- Associates
- Staff
- Entrepreneurs
- Manufacturers
- Friends

- Competitors
- Vendors
- Distributors
- Wholesalers
- Organization and industry Leaders

PLACES
- New offices
- Conventions
- Sales conferences
- Factories
- Airports
- Colleges
- Hotels

- Trade shows
- Workshops
- Retail outlets
- Cities
- Schools
- Training centers
- Car rentals

THINGS

- New products
- Cars
- Equipment
- Software
- Telecommunications
- Planes
- Natural resources
- Computers
- Electronics
- Inventions
- Hardware
- Trains
- Roads
- Business books

ACTIVITIES

- Industry events
- Training
- Selling
- Customer service
- Focus groups
- Meetings
- Ceremonies
- New business
- Prospecting
- Hiring
- Manufacturing
- Business travel
- Professional certification
- Fund-raising events

SITUATIONS

- Stock market
- Economic situations
- Legislation
- Demographics
- Business
- Rents
- Business climate
- Interest rates
- Safety
- Employment
- Internet issues
- Housing

CHALLENGES

- Low productivity
- Staffing
- Lower profits
- Wasted time
- Decreased sales
- High costs
- Customer complaints
- Government regulations
- Limited resources
- Fraud

Reminder for Competitive Networkers. Don't only zero in on specific words. In addition, listen carefully for the hidden information and implied meanings between the lines. Don't be overly literal or impatient and miss the feelings behind the words.

Reminder for Outgoing Networkers. Don't assume you know what people are going to say. Ask for clarification and seek a deeper understanding of their business issues and desired outcomes.

Reminder for Amiable Networkers. Don't be afraid to plunge deeper into a business discussion to uncover hidden or unresolved issues. Use follow-up questions to focus your inquiries.

Reminder for Analytical Networkers. Don't only listen for facts, mistakes, illogical conclusions, or sequences of events. In addition, acknowledge what you agree with and demonstrate your understanding of the overall desired outcomes by summarizing the "big picture."

Step 3: Refer to a Business-Related Keyword or Phrase

Make the transition from small talk to business by asking a question that refers to a keyword or topic related to business that you think the person is willing to discuss. For example:

- "You mentioned earlier that your company is expanding and needs more space. What kind of space are you looking for?"
- "You said you're starting a new project at work. I'm curious, what is it that you're doing?"
- "What's your area of expertise?"
- "What made you decide to go into that area?"
- "What are your company's plans for this year?"

- "How do you see your industry changing over the next year or so?"
- "Any interesting new projects coming up?"

In addition to carefully listening for little picture details (who, what, when, why, and where), look for big-picture implicit messages that suggest the person's overall level of receptivity, comfort, and trust. For example:

- Does his or her body language appear open or closed?
- Is he or she revealing more details than you asked for?
- Is he or she being overly cautious?
- Does he or she appear relaxed or nervous?
- What emotion is his or her voice expressing?

ENCOURAGE THE PROSPECT TO TALK MORE

Although you can let the person know if you have a particular interest or experience in that area or field, do not offer any unsolicited advice or solutions. That can come later. For now, listen carefully for wants, needs, goals, issues, and challenges. Your objective is to get the person to feel comfortable, open up, and reveal more information so you can determine whether he or she is a qualified prospect for you or someone you know.

Make mental notes of every keyword that you hear so you can refer to them later. Gently probe with more open-ended questions to encourage the prospect to open up and define the issues, problems, and goals in more detail. As he or she explains more, begin to prioritize needs and consider how your skills, experiences, or connections may provide solutions. The more a person talks, the more accurately you can identify areas where you may be able to offer some assistance in the form of your products, services, or contacts.

Reminder for Competitive Networkers. Gently ask the other person to elaborate on business-related topics.

Reminder for Outgoing Networkers. Focus follow-up questions and comments on business issues.

Reminder for Amiable Networkers. Steadily increase your level of participation in the conversation.

Reminder for Analytical Networkers. Show interest in all business-related topics, not just those that are technically based.

Step 4: Move the Conversation to Bigger Business Issues

Once you've established rapport with someone and have a better understanding of what the business issues might be, then it's time to make the transition from small talk about business to a big-deal discussion. Gently probe what you believe may be the person's bigger issues with questions such as:

- "What are your biggest challenges with that?"
- "Why is that a such a big problem?"
- "Why is that so critical to your business?"
- "What made you decide on that approach?"
- "In the best of all possible worlds, what would you like to happen?"
- "What's the worst thing that can happen if things don't go your way?"
- "What do you see as your options?"
- "If you had your choice, what option would be best for you?"
- "How is what you are doing now working for you?"

Reminder for Competitive Networkers. Don't hard sell or sound cold and calculated. Instead empathize, summarize the big picture, and articulate the major emotions related to the issues.

Reminder for Outgoing Networkers. Don't overwhelm the person with several ideas at once or hard sell your solutions. Instead check for understanding by restating main points and key details.

Reminder for Amiable Networkers. Don't let the other person dominate the conversation with complaints or pressure you to solve his or her problems. Stay actively involved and keep the conversation balanced between talking and listening.

Reminder for Analytical Networkers. Empathize, don't criticize the person's past efforts or offer unsolicited advice. Summarize the bigger picture and the emotions behind the facts and challenges.

Step 5: Link Your Capabilities to the Prospect's Needs

Once the person describes a specific big issue or problem that you or someone you know can address, *now is the time* to link your capabilities to his or her needs. The best way to do that without making it sound like a hard-sell pitch is to describe how you have helped other people solve similar problems or deal with similar issues. For example, you can say:

- "I helped a client in your industry do something similar a few months ago."
- "What a coincidence! I'm presently involved in a similar project."
- "That's interesting. You say that you need a . . . . I've been working in this industry for years."
- "I know a real pro who can help you with that."

The objective of these comments is to encourage the other person to ask you follow-up questions so that you have the opportunity to build your credibility. You can do this by offering some specific details—but not confidential information—about how you helped a client or two achieve their goals. If the prospect does *not* ask, then you can offer additional information by saying:

- "For example, I helped launch a . . . for XYZ Company. Now that was a challenge because . . . ."
- "My department just recently completed an energy-saving project for ABC Company that cut their costs by 10 percent. Is that something that would be a benefit to your company?"

Reminder for Competitive Networkers. Don't overstate your results or take all the credit. Instead, modestly describe how you and your team helped a client solve a similar problem and achieve a specific goal or outcome.

Reminder for Outgoing Networkers. Don't blow your own horn too loudly or for too long. Instead briefly and modestly describe how you helped a client solve a similar problem and achieve a specific goal or outcome.

Reminder for Amiable Networkers. Don't minimize your achievements. Explain your specific role in how you helped a client solve a similar problem and achieve a specific goal or outcome.

Reminder for Analytical Networkers. Avoid offering too many technical details, methods, or equipment that led to you and your team solving a similar problem or achieving a specific goal or outcome. Focus on how your clients benefited from you and your team's efforts.

Step 6: If You Get a "Buy Signal," Ask for an Appointment

How do you know if the person is considering doing business with you? One way is to listen for "buying signals." These are questions or comments about your experience, clients, fees, prices, or availability. For example:

- "Who are some of your other clients?"
- "What would you recommend that I do if I . . . ?"
- "May I ask you a professional question?"
- "You need to talk to our person in the . . . department."
- "How much do you charge?"

Of course, continue the conversation, but limit your suggestions or possible options. Never discuss money, your fees, or get into an extensive problem-solving mode at the networking event. Your next goal is to get an appointment so that you can discuss the idea of working together in private and in more detail. You can ask:

- "From what you described, this sounds like something I can help you with. May I call you tomorrow so we can discuss it in more detail? When is a good time to reach you?"
- "I'm wondering, is this something that you think I can help you with? If so, then let's make an appointment to meet and talk about it some more. Do you have your calendar handy?"
- "I'm happy to give you prices, but I really need to know more about your needs before I can give you an accurate quote."
- "If you're available, I can come by your office tomorrow morning or Thursday afternoon to discuss your project in more detail."

Reminder for All Networkers. Don't try to close a deal after getting a commitment for a follow-up meeting. Change topics and chat for a few minutes before closing the conversation. Then move on to another person or group.

END THE CONVERSATION AND LEAVE A GREAT LAST IMPRESSION

As your conversation comes to an end be sure to close it on a positive note, by doing the following before saying good-bye:

- Thank him or her for the opportunity to meet and talk.
- Restate when your next contact will be and who will initiate it.
- Briefly express your happiness at the possibility of doing business together.

Once your conversation is over, it is time to move on and talk to someone else at the event. Small talk has played its critical role in building rapport, determining a need, and establishing your credibility. You've met and qualified a new prospect, made a great impression, and set the stage for a big deal.

SMALL TALK PLAYS A BIG ROLE AND LEADS TO BIG DEALS

You've learned in this chapter how small talk is used to establish contact, build trust, create rapport, and boost credibility in an informal conversation. Once you have exchanged this critical information and transitioned to a mutually beneficial business discussion, you have moved a large step closer to a big deal.

11

Tactfully Escaping
Noxious Networkers

In this chapter you will learn how to:

- **Prevent annoying networkers from wasting your time**
- **Assertively deal with noxious networkers**
- **Stay cool and professional in challenging networking situations**
- **Tactfully end conversations with noxious networkers**

How many times have you found yourself in these kinds of unproductive conversations at networking events? You are talking to someone when the conversation suddenly turns into a diatribe about her company's unfair policies, lousy bosses, or poor management. You joined a conversation that turned into aggressive bantering about sports teams or political candidates. You get stuck listening to a bore's long-winded and often pointless stories. A competitor picks your brains to gather intelligence about your clients or company. And the list goes on and on. It's not that these noxious networkers are bad people. It's just that they can waste your valuable time with their litany of complaints, exaggerations, insecurities, and sometimes hostile behavior—but only if you let them.

ONE STRATEGY WILL NOT THWART ALL NOXIOUS NETWORKERS

You must be ready to adapt your escape strategies to each individual because what may improve the situation with one kind of noxious networker may only exacerbate it with another. You can effectively deal with most noxious networkers if you:

- Quickly spot them
- Identify their networking styles and adapt your strategies
- Avoid their tricks and traps
- Use assertive communication skills to minimize their negative impact
- Limit your time together—all while remaining polite and professional

> Deal with these noxious networkers and you will be more productive at networking events:
> ⊘ Know-it-alls ⊘ Chatterboxes ⊘ Complainers ⊘ Hitch-hikers ⊘ Gossips ⊘ Sharks

DEALING WITH KNOW-IT-ALLS AT NETWORKING EVENTS

We've all been in conversations at networking events with people who think they know everything and constantly challenge or disagree with just about everything we say, especially in front of others. Before we finish making our point, they interrupt us with aggressive challenges such as "Prove it!" or "Says who?"

Know-it-alls approach conversations at networking events as competitions with winners and losers. They are out to win conversations by challenging your credibility and making themselves look good at your expense. It's a clear signal that Know-it-alls are about to challenge your views in a group conversation when they folds their arms, tilt their head back to one side, and then thrust their chins outward. Your suspicions will quickly be confirmed when they sling arrows with, "I don't think so!" or "Wrong!"

But don't fall for this trap, because the moment you respond to the challenge, they will continue their campaign to discredit you by turning up one corner of their mouths in contempt, rolling their eyes upward, or waving their hands as if shooing away a fly. And, if that's not enough to provoke you into an argument, then they'll grunt, groan, or yawn to communicate disbelief, disagreement, or boredom. Finally, you'll be subjected to their exaggerated sense of self-importance with a lecture or a condescending comment such as "I think I know a little bit more about that subject than you do" or "I think that's a bit naive, don't you?"

Assertive Strategy: Disagree, but Don't Argue

Know-it-alls pick and win arguments, not because they are always right, but because they are confident they can win by ridiculing, intimidating, or bullying people with whom they disagree. Even if you can soundly beat back the challenge, it is almost always a complete waste of your valuable networking time to get into debates or long conversations with a Know-it-alls. True, you may win the battles and put Know-it-alls in their place, but it is highly unlikely that they will ever become clients or refer any business to you. Plus, Know-it-alls will only continue debating without you to others. Therefore, it's best to avoid debates by saying something like:

- "I have a different view of the situation."
- "My experience is different than what you describe."
- "I don't think this is the time or place to get into a debate about that."

Escape Strategy: Acknowledge Differences—Then Make Your Getaway

At this point, your patience may be growing thin, so it's probably a good time to end the conversation and move on, but you need to do so politely and professionally. Here's what you can say to excuse yourself from the conversation: Use the Know-it-all's name, make about five seconds of eye contact, and give a firm handshake, then say, "It's been interesting chatting with you, but obviously we see things quite differently. Let's just agree to disagree. I want to say hello to some other people here, so please excuse me. Enjoy the rest of your evening."

Reminder for Analytical Networkers. Although you may be right about an issue or specific point, getting into debates with Know-it-alls at networking events will only waste your time.

DEALING WITH CHATTERBOXES AT NETWORKING EVENTS

Chatterboxes are bubbly people who seem to talk nonstop and attend networking events more for social reasons than anything else. They rarely network with any specific goal, but prefer to spend most of their time at these events jabbering about their personal lives or matters that have little relevance to your business. Chatterboxes are easy to spot because they monopolize the conversation with their stories and antics. They gesture with their arms and hands and use facial expressions to overemphasize their role in an event or story. They stand near enough to touch the arms or shoulders of those they talk to, whether they are in groups or in one-on-one conversations.

Chatterboxes can talk so rapidly that it's hard to get a word in edgewise, even as they ramble from subject to subject. If someone does manage to offer a comment, Chatterboxes will likely interrupt and keep on talking. Silence in a conversation makes them feel very uncomfortable, so they are always ready to fill in the void with their favorite subject—themselves!

Assertive Strategy: Stop Their Flow of Words—Then Grab the Conversational Ball and Don't Let Go

If you let Chatterboxes monopolize the conversation, it's all over. Instead, after politely listening for a minute or so, interrupt and break their monologue with several closed-ended "who-what-when-where" or yes-no questions. For example, "Who was there?" "What was it for?" "When did this happen?" "Where was it?" "Did you say five or seven?"

Having to answer several closed-ended questions will force Chatterboxes to slow down, but not stop talking entirely. That's why at this point you must take control. Immediately after their response to your third or fourth question, grab the conversational ball and keep it by introducing and talking about a new business-related subject. For example, "I see. Before I forget, I need to tell you one very important thing about our organization's plans for our next annual meeting."

You can maintain control by referring to the networking event, your organization, other attendees, or your reasons for attending the function. Be sure to keep talking and don't ask Chatterboxes any questions or they will be right back talking a mile a minute. If Chatterboxes interrupt you, don't let them talk for more than a few sentences before you interject "Hold on! Wait a minute! Let me finish." Then reassert yourself as the one directing the conversation.

Escape Strategy: Guide the Conversation to a Business Topic—Then Send an Exit Signal

Once you have shifted the balance of the conversation, send your "exit signal" by announcing that you only have a little more time to talk before moving on. For example:

- "I want to tell you one more thing before I run off and say hello to some other people."

Of course, as in all encounters at networking events, end your conversations on a positive note with the person's name, a warm smile, a handshake, and something like:

- "I'm glad we got a chance to chat. Enjoy the rest of the event."

Reminder for Amiable Networkers. You are being assertive, not impolite, when you interrupt Chatterboxes and take control of the conversation.

DEALING WITH COMPLAINERS AT NETWORKING EVENTS

The body language of Complainers says it all! They stand with their arms folded across their chests, one hand covering their mouths. Their chins are tucked inward and their eyes downcast toward their feet. They glance from side to side, and then upward briefly looking into your eyes to see if the "poor me" message has generated any sympathy. "Everyone else has all the luck. I just can't seem to get a break!" or "I guess I just don't know the right people!" are the woeful words of Complainers explaining why things are not going their way.

Complainers at networking events are *not* looking for business, but instead are hoping to find people who will listen to their litany of excuses and offer them a sympathetic ear. It's not that you don't care about others or that you are unwilling to help people who are going through a rough patch—you *do* care and will do what you can for others. And it's true that people have serious medical problems or family issues that can interfere with their business and lives. However, no one at networking events can afford to or wants to spend their limited time listening to the problems of Complainers.

Assertive Strategy: Sympathize—Then Change Topics

If you let Complainers grouse about their problems, you'll be trapped for who knows how long. On the other hand, if you ignore their feelings you'll appear cold or uncaring. Therefore, after politely listening for a minute or so, paraphrase the conversation to show that you are listening. Then sincerely offer a few kind words and firmly take charge of the conversation by changing topics. This will send a clear signal that you want to talk about something else. For example, you can say something like:

- "I'm sorry to hear about you losing that contact. I agree that business is very tough right now, but I hope things improve for you. Speaking of which, I read an inspiring article in the business section about an entrepreneur who . . . ."

Escape Strategy: Discuss an Upbeat Topic—Then Make Your Getaway

The challenge in talking to Complainers is keeping the conversation from regressing to problems—theirs or yours. One way to do that is to bring up an inspiring, heartwarming, or motivating topic that both of you can talk about. After discussing a more positive topic for a few minutes, send a signal that you are ready to close your conversation. Do so without referring to any prior negative issues. You can say something like, "It's been nice chatting with you about . . . (positive topic)." Then smile, shake hands, use his or her name and say, "I'm going to say hello to some other people at the event before the program begins. Enjoy the rest of the day."

Reminder for Outgoing Networkers. Strictly limit the time you spend with Complainers or you will get trapped into talking about their problems.

DEALING WITH HITCHHIKERS AT NETWORKING EVENTS

Hitchhikers are shy people who latch on to other people at networking events with whom they feel comfortable, and they remain with them for as long as possible. The body language of Hitchhikers can look like that of other noxious networkers— arms folded across the chest, possibly a hand covering the mouth or chin, and little eye contact. This can make Hitchhikers appear distracted, worried, awkward, and shy.

If a stranger does enter the conversation, Hitchhikers won't say much because they are usually intimidated or uncomfortable meeting strangers. If asked a question they will respond, but their responses will probably be limited to a few words spoken in soft, hesitating, and monotone voices. If the "friends" try to close the conversation and move toward others in the room, Hitchhikers will tag along. Hitchhikers may be nice people, but having one by your side for an entire event can hamper your ability to work the room, make it difficult to contact a target prospect and speak to him or her one-on-one, and it may scare away other networkers attracted to you.

Assertive Strategy: Build Their Confidence—Let Them Know You Network Solo

Hitchhikers can become more independent networkers if you first offer them confidence-building statements that highlight their abilities and then reinforce how they and others can benefit from networking. You can say something like:

- "You are one of the few people I've met who truly knows how to . . . . I know several people here that I want to introduce you to who can really use your help. Would you like to meet them?"

Make it clear without being harsh that you prefer to network solo. You can say:

- "I find working the room alone allows me to meet more people at these events so please don't be offended if I trot off and chat with several other people in a few minutes."

Escape Strategy: Introduction and Exit

After a few minutes of chatting, politely make it clear that your conversation is coming to an end by saying:

- "I've enjoyed talking to you, but it's time for me to say good-bye and meet some new people. But before I do, I see someone at the refreshment table that I want to introduce you to. Walk over there with me."

At that point, you probably have a good opportunity to introduce the Hitchhiker to other people attending the event, and then make your move to another person or group. However, if the Hitchhiker continues to follow you, you can gently say:

- "Would you mind excusing me? I want a few minutes alone to talk to someone."

Reminder for Competitive Networkers. Giving a little extra time and help to technically oriented Hitchhikers will pay off in the future when you need help from them.

DEALING WITH GOSSIPS AT NETWORKING EVENTS

"Don't tell anyone I told you this, but . . . ." Secrets, rumors, innuendo, and confidential information are the stock-in-trade of Gossips at networking events. Gossips want attention and they use what they consider as special knowledge or inside information to make themselves appear important. Gossips waste your time at networking events, not only because they disseminate unreliable information, but also because they have few truly valuable contacts to share.

Gossips use their closed body language to reinforce that what they have to say is confidential. Like Hitchhikers, they may fold their arms or place one hand near their mouths or chins, but for a different reason—they want to appear cunning. They lean closer to the person or people they are talking to so no one else can hear what they're saying. Gossips raise their eyebrows and turn down the corners of their mouths suggesting they are privileged enough to know special secrets. Gossips are usually soft-spoken because they don't want everyone to know the source of any unbecoming comments or personal or confidential information.

Assertive Strategy: Show No Interest—Change Topics

Nip gossip in the bud as soon as you hear the first words about the personal lives of others or a company's confidential information. If you let Gossips think for a second that you're interested, you'll be trapped and possibly accused by them of actually requesting information. Simply say, "Actually, I couldn't care less."

Another trick Gossips play is pumping others for confidential information or "juicy tidbits" about coworkers, bosses, clients, or customers, promising you that whatever you tell them will remain a secret. Don't get sucked into this ruse. Just say: "No, that's confidential" or "What happens at work stays at work."

Escape Strategy: Change Topics—Then Change Seats

After you show a lack of interest in the tattle or probing Gossips, change the topic to something related to your industry or the event. Afterward, you can excuse yourself from the conversation by saying something like, "What I am interested in is this presentation. I think this seat is a little too far away for me so I'm going to move a bit closer. Enjoy the meeting."

DEALING WITH SHARKS AT NETWORKING EVENTS

Sharks are superaggressive networkers whose business philosophy boils down to this: "What can you do for *me*?" Sharks use as little time as possible at networking events to find out 1) who you are, 2) who you know, and 3) if you want to buy their product or service. If they think that you will buy something from them, introduce them to someone important, help them get ahead, or benefit in some way, then they will treat you like you are their best friend. However, if they determine you have little to offer them, then they will drop you like a hot potato.

At a networking event sharks are always moving from person to person, group to group, spending at times less than a minute or two with the people they meet. However, when Sharks do stop to talk to you, they engage you face-to-face, as they scrutinizes and judge whether you are worthy of a few minutes more of their time. Meanwhile, their eyes glance constantly over your shoulder, scanning the room looking for someone more important than you to talk to.

Sharks are serious and deliberate networkers. They avoid small talk and get right to business with short, often colorless questions designed to qualify people from the very beginning of the conversation. For example:

- "Who do you work for and what do you do?"
- "Let me get right to the point. Are you interested in buying . . . ?"
- "If I could show you a way to double your results, would you be interested?"
- "Who do you know here that's a decision-maker?"

Assertive Strategy: Be Direct and Firm

The fastest way to minimize contact with Sharks at networking events is simply to be direct and say, "I'm not your market or customer. I'm sure someone else would be a much better prospect for what you have to offer."

Escape Strategy: Politely Close the Conversation— Excuse Yourself

Sharks are relentless and if they smell a sale or see you as a potential asset or contact to a decision-maker, they may try to pressure you into a follow-up appointment, an introduction, or even an on-the-spot hard-sell. Don't let Sharks bully you into anything at networking events, and don't worry that your rejection will cause hurt feelings. Just say something like, "Excuse me, I don't want you to waste your time, and I'm definitely not interested. Now if you'll excuse me, I must say hello to one of the other guests before she leaves."

STAY PROFESSIONAL, ASSERTIVE, AND READY TO MOVE ON

In this chapter you learned that the key to handling Know-it-alls, Chatterboxes, Complainers, Hitchhikers, Gossips, and Sharks is to assertively take control of conversations without losing your cool or professionalism. If you follow the advice given here, you'll never lose valuable time at networking events to these noxious networkers. You can then engage those people who are more likely to lead you to a big deal.

12

Ten Ways to Follow Up That Lead to Big Deals

In this chapter you will learn how to:

- **Reinforce positive first impressions with new contacts**
- **Strengthen rapport, trust, and credibility with new contacts**
- **Stay in touch with new contacts**
- **Build long-term relationships with contacts that can lead to big deals**

You've used the guest list to help you target prospects and remember names at a networking event. You've also collected lots of business cards and chatted up other attendees about your latest product or service. However, if you are like many networkers, myself included, follow-up is the weakest part of your networking efforts. Yet all of us acknowledge that it is the most important thing to do after making a contact at an event. Of course, bombarding new contacts with unsolicited offers or useless information will make an impression, but probably not the kind that will win you new clients or sales! Here are tips on how to follow up after a networking event with new contacts that will sustain a positive impression and can lead to big deals in the future.

FOLLOWING UP AFTER A NETWORKING EVENT TURNS CONTACTS INTO CLIENTS

Tip #1: Follow Up Within a Week

Tip #2: Promptly Send Articles, Information, Samples, or Gifts You Promised

Tip #3: Ask for an Appointment

Tip #4: Invite a Contact for Coffee or an Informal Meal

Tip #5: Invite a Contact to Join You at an Industry-Related Event

Tip #6: Invite a Contact to a Leisure Activity

Tip #7: Offer New Contacts Referrals to Other Vendors

Tip #8: Refer Business Opportunities to Your Contacts

Tip #9: Show Your Appreciation with a Small Gift or Classy Meal

Tip #10: Maintain Regular Contact

TIP #1: FOLLOW UP WITHIN A WEEK

Following up soon after a networking event demonstrates a sense of importance and immediacy—traits that most serious businesspeople like and value. A timely follow-up shows you do not procrastinate, signals that you believe there is a mutual benefit to building the relationship, and allows you to express your appreciation if he or she introduced you to a potential client or useful contact.

Your Follow-Up Can Be an E-mail, a Handwritten Note, or a Telephone Call

Following up reinforces the connection you made in person and gives you the opportunity to suggest an additional meeting or conversation. Whether you send e-mails or handwritten notes make sure they are well written and free of spelling and grammatical errors. Remember your goal is to make a good impression, and sloppy writing—even in e-mails—does not present a picture of someone who pays attention to details.

If you want your follow-up to be even more personal, make a short telephone call. Always reintroduce yourself, identify where you met, ask if it's a convenient time to chat for a minute, and have a question ready to ask. If you do have the opportunity to chat, then you can discuss the event or another business topic in more detail. If your conversation continues more than a few minutes, suggest a follow-up call or meeting to continue your discussion. That way you can take the converstion to the next level because you've got more time to talk.

Reminder to Competitive and Outgoing Networkers. Focus your follow-up conversation based on your previous contact, not on a canned sales pitch.

TIP #2: PROMPTLY SEND ARTICLES, INFORMATION, SAMPLES, OR GIFTS YOU PROMISED

Most networkers are grateful and impressed when someone at a networking event offers them useful information and they actually receive it within a few days. If you include additional sales materials, be sure that they appear secondary to the materials or information you promised or it will look like a bait-and-switch gimmick. Again, the sooner you send requested information the better—the longer you wait, the less impact it will have.

Reminder to Analytical Networkers. Don't do a data dump on your new contact. Only send information relevant to your conversation.

TIP #3: ASK FOR AN APPOINTMENT

Of course, if you get a direct request from someone who wants to learn more about your products or services, then by all means ask for the appointment. You can use a trial close such as "Is this something you'd like to talk about some more?" If he or she answers yes, then say, "Let's get our calendars out and make an appointment to talk again, say early next week?" Sometimes it may take a few follow-up contacts before both parties agree to meet again.

Reminder to Amiable Networkers. Taking the risk to ask for the appointment shows you are confident and goal oriented.

TIP #4: INVITE A CONTACT FOR COFFEE OR AN INFORMAL MEAL

Most people need more than one conversation at a networking event to build enough trust, rapport, and confidence in each other's abilities to enter into a business relationship or refer a client. One of the best ways to strengthen a new relationship is over a cup of coffee or an informal meal. Sharing time this way allows you to get to know each other better, exchange experiences, discuss your respective businesses, and determine how you might help each other achieve your goals. Remember two things:

1) this is not a sales call—it's a rapport-building meeting, and 2) if you offer the invitation, you pay for the meal.

Reminder to Amiable and Analytical Networkers. Engaging potential clients in one-on-one business conversations allows you more time to build rapport, understand issues, establish credibility, and reveal your areas of expertise.

TIP #5: INVITE A CONTACT TO JOIN YOU AT AN INDUSTRY-RELATED EVENT

Inviting a contact to join you at an industry-related event shows that you have common interests and gives you an opportunity to see where your skills and those of your contact overlap or are different. Most serious businesspeople are open to this kind of follow-up, but you must match the program with the interests of the particular individual.

Reminder to Outgoing Networkers. Attending business events with potential clients will enhance your professional image and underscore an aligned approach to business issues.

TIP #6: INVITE A CONTACT TO A LEISURE ACTIVITY

When my father worked as a plant engineer, he used to whistle "Take Me Out to the Ball Game" whenever a particular equipment salesman would visit him on the job. This salesman knew that mixing in a bit of leisure activity was good for business. If it is appropriate, consider inviting a contact to join you for a professional sports event, golf outing, concert, or some other leisure activity you think he or she will enjoy. The purpose of sharing a leisure activity is to get to know each other better and to talk about a variety of topics, some of which may include business, but does not have to. The informal conversation lends itself to opening up and sharing more information, thus building and deepening the business relationship.

Reminder to All Networkers. When you mix business and pleasure, it's still mostly about business.

TIP #7: OFFER NEW CONTACTS REFERRALS TO OTHER VENDORS

Most businesspeople agree that finding good vendors is an ongoing challenge, so if you can refer proven vendors to new contacts, then your value to both will increase. However, never refer anyone you cannot personally vouch for. A referral who disappoints a new contact will surely spoil the relationship. If you help a new contact, he or she will see you as a resource, someone who cares about helping others, who understands reciprocal relationships, and someone who, if the opportunity presents itself, deserves a referral.

TIP #8: REFER BUSINESS OPPORTUNITIES TO YOUR CONTACTS

"I have a referral for you." Those are the six magic words that every networker wants to hear and that will turn a new contact into a solid business relationship. Of course, referrals must be offered with care. Make sure that the potential client is legitimate and worthy of your new contact's time and trouble. If everything works out for both, then everyone will be happy, because now two people will be likely to reciprocate by passing on referrals to you.

Reminder to All Networkers. What you give out you get back.

TIP #9: SHOW YOUR APPRECIATION WITH A SMALL GIFT OR CLASSY MEAL

While you certainly don't need to send every networking contact a gift, if someone has been especially helpful to you or if he or she is a client whose loyalty you want to reward, then consider sending a suitable gift. What is suitable? That depends entirely upon the client and your budget. What's important is that you show others that you appreciate who they are and what they have done for you.

TIP #10: MAINTAIN REGULAR CONTACT

Even if key contacts haven't recently given you any business or sent you a referral, networking experts suggest reaching out to these people several times a year. Call with an invitation to a networking event; e-mail a book, movie, or restaurant review; send a postcard from your favorite vacation spot; or forward an e-zine newsletter with the latest industry news. For example, you might write something like, "Dear . . . How have you been? I recently read an article about . . . (ate in . . . restaurant, etc.) and I thought of you! It's been a few months since we've talked. Let's catch up on what's new."

Remember that timing is everything and you never know when your e-mail, call, or newsletter might arrive just when your services or products are most needed.

FOLLOW-UP + IMPACT = MORE BUSINESS WITH NETWORKERS

You've learned in this chapter that following up in a timely fashion pays off and helps build business relationships. Making follow-up contact within a week keeps impressions strong and contacts warm. Following up implies that the person you met was important, and your "thank you" note shows that you value his or her efforts on your behalf. Perhaps, most important, following up soon after an event creates an impression that you like him or her and that you see potential for a business relationship. It should then come as no surprise that every contact you make at a networking event will probably think of you first when the opportunity for business in your area comes up.

Twelve Common Networking Mistakes and How to Correct Them

In this chapter you will learn how to:

- **Identify and correct the most common networking mistakes**
- **Refocus your networking efforts for better results**
- **Better connect with other networkers**
- **Project a professional image to everyone you meet**

Are you spending time, effort, and money networking at lots of business and social functions, but not seeing tangible results? If the time you spend networking is not paying off the way you want, then you may be committing one or more of the 12 most common networking pitfalls. Once you identify your networking mistakes, make the recommended corrections and watch the results from your networking increase.

112

MISTAKE #1: ATTENDING TOO MANY UNPRODUCTIVE NETWORKING EVENTS

When it comes to attending networking events, more is not always better, especially if your networking calendar is filled with too many events that give you little return on your investment of time, effort, and energy. Outgoing Networkers may be more prone to this mistake because they think more activity yields more results.

Correction. Only attend networking events that have the highest likelihood of a payoff. Use a more focused approach by prioritizing potential events based on who is attending, when and where the events take place, and the potential for you to accomplish one or more specific networking goals.

MISTAKE #2: NOT DOING BACKGROUND RESEARCH BEFORE THE NETWORKING EVENT

If you claim you don't have the time to do background research on the companies, vendors, and key individuals before you attend networking events, then consider this: Not doing your homework will waste your valuable time because it will increase the likelihood of you missing golden opportunities and losing out to your more proactive competitors. Competitive and Outgoing Networkers are prone to this mistake because they are used to impressing people with their charisma and personality.

Correction. You don't have to do a search on everyone attending an event, but spending an hour or so to find out about breaking industry news, the hottest deals, and the latest personnel changes can pay off big when you network.

MISTAKE #3: ATTENDING NETWORKING EVENTS WITH TOO MANY COMPETITORS

Of course, it's good to network at your industry's trade shows and association meetings. However, if your competitors and vendors frequently outnumber your prospects at these events then it will be more difficult for you to find and capture the attention of potential clients or customers in these venues. Amiable and Analytical Networkers may be more prone to this mistake because they feel much more comfortable with people they know and with whom they share interests and experiences.

Correction. Attend the trade shows, conventions, and association meetings of the different professions and people who use, or could use, your products and services. Chances are, you will be outnumbered by potential customers instead of competitors, and the likelihood of you connecting with qualified prospects will improve considerably.

MISTAKE #4: BEING UNAWARE OF CURRENT INDUSTRY CHANGES

"You don't know that . . . was sold to . . . ? Where have you been? It's been all over the news!" Not keeping up-to-date on the latest news, personnel changes, and company realignments in your industry can leave you looking embarrassed, unprofessional, and behind the times. Amiable Networkers and Analytical Networkers are prone to this mistake because they tend to stay focused on the details of current projects rather than on the industry's big picture.

Correction. In addition to at least scanning the business sections of the major newspapers and magazines, be sure to carefully read your trade publications for the latest hirings, firings, promotions, surveys, projections, stock market quotations, and other critical information in your markets and related to your customers and prospects.

MISTAKE #5: NO KNOWLEDGE OF THE ORGANIZATION SPONSORING THE EVENT

How often do you attend networking events hosted by organizations that you know next to nothing about? The less you know about an organization's officers and its mission statement or membership, the more uninformed and unprepared you look. Prospects and members are rarely impressed with people who know little about their organization. Analytical Networkers may be more prone to this mistake because they tend to undervalue the organization and overvalue its products or processes.

Correction. Finding out basic information about an organization, association, or business is as easy as typing the name into your favorite search engine and looking at what comes up. First, visit its Web site and read the mission statement. Next, check the membership page, see who the leaders are and if you know anyone in the organization. Finally, visit a few of the other links that come up in your search, particularly ones that refer to recent articles. In 15 to 30 minutes you can find most of what you need to know, including the organization's leaders, goals, recent publicity, and upcoming events. Then when somebody brings one of those topics up in conversation you'll sound informed about and interested in the organization.

MISTAKE #6: NOT DONATING SAMPLES OR FREE CONSULTING AS RAFFLE ITEMS

Have you ever won a free book, an audio program, a product, a consultation, or some other prize at a networking event? If you have, you probably felt pretty good about what you won and about the company, organization, or person who gave it to you. Where do you think those items come from? None other than organization members, guests, or vendors who want to curry favor with prospects. If you're not one of those wise marketers who knows the value of a "free gift," then you are missing an inexpensive and hugely effective opportunity to generate lots of publicity and goodwill. Any networker who equates "free" with "no value" is missing the boat on this one.

Correction. Be generous with your *top* products and services by offering them as giveaways at meetings and fund-raising events that your prospects attend. (Closeouts or substandard products will earn you little gratitude and no new business.) When you attend the event and give away the items yourself, prospects will see you and your company as caring about the organization and wanting to help its members. As a result, when prospects are looking to purchase a particular product or service that you offer, they will likely remember your generosity and give you a call.

MISTAKE #7: VAGUELY DESCRIBING WHAT YOU DO

How you answer, "What do you do?" can make the difference between a contact engaging you in conversation or quickly excusing him or herself and moving on to talk to someone else in the room. If your answer is a long complicated explanation, they'll never get it. On the other hand, if you offer just a one- or two-word description such as "I'm a consultant" or "I'm an attorney," people will stereotype you with others in that profession. And you'll only leave people confused about what you do if you try to sound mysterious with vaguely worded phrases such as "I give people their roadmap to financial independence" or "I am involved in a new way to market a unique new idea that will result in financial success." Competitive, Amiable, and Analytical Networkers are prone to using official job titles that often lead to stereotyping, while Outgoing Networkers may spout wordy descriptions that offer little insight into how they earn their living.

Correction. Briefly describe what you do and give people enough concrete information so that they can easily tell others how you can help them. For example, I frequently answer that question with this simple response: "I write books and give workshops on how to break the ice and make small talk pay off in social and business situations." Here are a few more examples of how to answer, "What do you do?"

- "I'm an attorney who helps small businesses to . . . ."
- "I help companies find the right people for the right jobs."
- "Our company creates and sells products that help . . . ."

MISTAKE #8: NOT DISTINGUISHING YOURSELF FROM YOUR COMPETITORS

"We already have a supplier for that" is a common phrase most vendors hear when networking for new prospects. However, most likely your prospects have little idea of how you and your competitor's products or services compare to one another, other than by price. Without differentiating yourself and the benefits of your products or services from those of your competitors, they will probably not consider you as an alternative or supplement to their existing vendors. Amiable Networkers may be prone to this mistake because they prefer to play it safe with "the norm" rather than risk standing out with something different.

Correction. Simply explain how you and your products or services offer different benefits than your competitors'. This allows prospects to focus on what you have to offer and how it can improve their situations in relation to their existing vendors.

MISTAKE #9: CRITICIZING YOUR COMPETITORS

Although it is tactless and unprofessional to criticize competitors behind their backs at networking events, people seem to do it all the time. The problem is that sooner or later crass comments will almost always get back to rivals. When that happens, someone who may have been a friendly competitor will certainly become a hostile adversary. Then prepare yourself for an embarrassing confrontation or clumsy apology at a future event. Competitive and Analytical Networkers are prone to boosting their products or services by knocking their competition. However, if you denigrate someone's vendor, you in effect, are saying that the prospect made a poor buying decision. This will not win you any new business.

Correction. When you attend networking events, keep all negative opinions about your competitors to yourself and never highlight their personal shortcomings as a way of enhancing your image to others. If you do compare your products and services to your competitors', do so in a way that defines and emphasizes the differences in their features and benefits.

MISTAKE # 10: TREATING COMPETITORS AS ADVERSARIES

Every person in business wants to win customers over their competitors. However, if you consider your competition as an adversary, then not only does that limit your relationship to one of a winner and loser, but it can make for uncomfortable and stressful conversations at industry-related networking events. Competitive and Analytical Networkers may be prone to this mistake because they tend to focus more on winning and being right than on building lasting professional relationships.

Correction. Compete by offering the best products and services you can through advertising, direct marketing, and promotion. Define your business relationship as "friendly competitors" so you can call upon one another for assistance, information, or support. That way, you'll have a lot more fun and a lot less stress at networking events that are attended by your competitors.

MISTAKE #11: IGNORING OTHERS SEATED AT YOUR TABLE

It's common at networking events for people to find themselves seated at a round or rectangular table with 8 to 10 strangers as they wait for the program to begin. Typically, most people will chat with the folks seated on either side of them, and give nothing more to others at the table than a cursory nod of recognition. What could signal more disinterest or unfriendliness? Amiable and Analytical Networkers are prone to this mistake because they might think that others will see their overtures as too forward or pushy.

Correction. At least several minutes before the program begins, politely break off the conversations with the people next to you, stand, and say, "I want to meet everyone at the table before we get started." Then move from person to person, introducing yourself and, as time permits, engaging as many as you can in a brief conversation. If that doesn't show you are confident, friendly, and interested in making contact with those seated around you, I don't know what does!

MISTAKE #12: NOT HELPING OTHERS MAKE CONNECTIONS

Yes, networking is a "numbers game" and the more people you meet the better. However, are you using your contacts to the greatest possible advantage for the greatest number of people you meet? If you're not introducing plenty of your contacts to one another, then you are ignoring the important strategic networking goal of positioning yourself as a resource to others. Networkers who are prone to this will give the impression that they are networking only for their own personal gain.

Correction. Remember that a primary networking goal is to help others connect. So, when you meet someone at a networking event who you think can benefit from an introduction to one of the other attendees you know, don't close your conversation before bringing the two together. If your contact is not at the event, tell your new acquaintance that you'll e-mail or call him or her with your contact's information. If it is a good match, then both people will be beholden to you, and hopefully, return the favor in the form of an introduction or a referral.

TURN SMALL NETWORKING MISTAKES INTO BIG BUSINESS OPPORTUNITIES

Now that you have learned common networking mistakes and how to correct them, look for other areas where you can fine-tune your business-related conversations. Maximize your networking opportunities by adapting to different networking styles, utilizing pre-event strategies, using small-talk techniques, dealing with noxious networkers, and applying follow-up tips. You're now ready to put all these elements into practice in the next three parts of this book: Opening Lines, Topics, and Networking Strategies in Business, Social, and Public Situations.

PART III

BUSINESS SITUATIONS: OPENING LINES, TOPICS, AND NETWORKING STRATEGIES

14

Four Rules of Networking Etiquette in Business Situations

In this chapter you will learn:

- **Conversational preferences of the four networking styles in business situations**
- **Four basic rules of networking etiquette in business situations**
- **How to avoid embarrassing conversations and comments in business situations**

Peter Post, director of the Emily Post Institute, probably said it best: "Your skills can get you in the door; your people skills are what can seal the deal." Of course, there are many guidelines governing etiquette, but if you think all you need to worry about at a business conference is which fork to use at dinner, then think again! First you need to know the conversational preferences of the four networking styles in business situations so you will know what to say and what not to say to avoid quickly scuttling your chances of making a big deal. Next, you need to know the four rules of networking etiquette in business situations.

Let's start with the conversational preferences in business situations of the four networking styles.

Competitive Networkers are most comfortable in business situations because most conversation topics are related to money, commerce, and entrepreneurship. Use questions or phrases that focus on vision such as "Tell me where you see our business going in the next few years" or "What's your next big project?" Avoid overly personal topics or ones that focus on emotions and feelings.

Outgoing Networkers are generally comfortable in business situations, but may come across as "all talk and no action" if they chatter too much or try too hard to be the center of attention. Avoid using negative phrases such as "Isn't it terrible that . . . ?" or solemn topics with Outgoing Networkers in business situations because overly serious topics make them uncomfortable and they will lose interest in the conversation.

Amiable Networkers can feel shy or even intimidated in unfamiliar business situations, so it is best to approach them in a way that somewhat matches their energy and demeanor. When talking to Amiable Networkers, avoid confrontational phrases such as "Don't you think that . . . ?" or "Why not?" Instead, use questions that begin with "How do you feel about . . . ?" or phrases such as "I'd love to know your opinion of . . . ."

Analytical Networkers can feel inhibited in unfamiliar business situations until the topic turns to their area of expertise—then they are in their element. However, avoid challenging their facts, opinions, or conclusions, as they can be quite competitive and will "fight rather than switch" views. When talking to Analytical Networkers encourage them to share their opinions with flattering phrases such as "You certainly have a lot of experience in this area. I'd like to know what do you think about . . . ."

Next you need to know the following four rules while networking in a business situation.

1. FOCUS ON BUSINESS TOPICS BUT ALSO BE WILLING TO MAKE SMALL TALK

Most people expect to discuss business-related issues and topics when they network in business situations, so it would be poor etiquette to disappoint them. At the same time, the best networkers are those people who are flexible enough to converse about a variety of topics before or after a business discussion. The correct etiquette as it pertains to first making small talk or discussing business depends on a person's networking style, preference, and the specific conversation. Competitive and Analytical Networkers need to pay particular attention to this rule, or others will see them as self-serving individuals only interested in talking to people who can help them make money.

2. DO NOT MONOPOLIZE ONE PERSON'S TIME

All skilled networkers know that they have a limited amount of time to devote to any one individual at a networking event. Therefore, trapping a prospective client into an unwelcome lengthy sales pitch is generally considered poor networking etiquette. Likewise, don't be offended if someone you are talking to closes your conversation after a few minutes to work the room and meet someone else. Amiable and Analytical Networkers need to pay particular attention to this rule or others may see them as insecure about mixing and mingling with strangers.

3. DO NOT PASS OUT MARKETING MATERIALS UNLESS SOMEONE ASKS FOR THEM

It is usually considered poor networking etiquette to hand out unsolicited marketing materials at an event. If someone asks for your marketing materials, request a business card, make a note on the back to mail the materials, and promise that they will arrive within the week following the event. Or, if your company is a vendor at the event, request the prospect's card and guide the person to your booth before you offer the materials. Competitive Networkers need to pay particular attention to this rule, or they will come across to others as only sales focused.

4. DO NOT DISCUSS POLITICS OR CONTROVERSIAL SUBJECTS

Although this wise and traditional advice is common sense, I am constantly amazed at how many people ignore it at networking events. Sure, you may find discussing politics or controversial issues interesting, but the problem is that when people do not share a point of view in these areas, there's a strong likelihood that they will create a negative impression of one another. As a result, you'll probably be passed over as a resource or contact, no matter how good a product or service you have to offer.

FOLLOWING NETWORKING ETIQUETTE IN BUSINESS SITUATIONS BUILDS YOUR CREDIBILITY FOR BIG DEALS

In this chapter you learned that when networking in business situations too much small talk, glib remarks, hard sells, or monopolizing another person's time at a networking event usually turns off other businesspeople. When you avoid these pitfalls, your credibility will increase, and other professionals will be more likely to consider big deals with you more seriously. Now you are ready to learn how to apply these rules of etiquette to networking in common business situations.

15

Trade Shows and Conferences

Strategic networking at trade shows and conferences gives you the opportunity to meet perspective customers, vendors, colleagues, business reps, sales managers, and some owners and executives while researching industry trends firsthand. Just strolling past innumerable booths of current and emerging products and services will give you all the inspiration for opening lines that you'll ever need. In addition, you can introduce yourself and your company to the suppliers, reps, and sales executives from large and small companies attending the show.

SOCIAL NETWORKING FOR EVENT PLANNERS AND ATTENDEES

Are you planning, promoting, or attending a convention or trade show? If you are a meeting planner, an attendee, a speaker, a vendor, hotel sales reps or anyone else in-

---

volved with the gigantic conference industry, then log on to any of the many specialized or "mega" social networking sites leading the way into this lucrative market. While sophistication and services vary, the larger sites offer members the latest industry news and information for the meeting, convention, incentive, and trade show professionals while featuring searchable article archives, crucial business resources, workflow tools, live webinars, and much more.

In addition, attendees can find information about other attendees, speakers, and special programs as well as networking events taking place around the conference. Some sites also include a database sorted by industries, regions, and dates of major conferences, conventions, and trade shows with social networking tools designed to increase attendee contacts along with their overall experience.

To find more about trade shows and conferences near you, type: *social networking + industry + trade shows + your city* into your favorite search engine.

TOPICS THAT MOST NETWORKERS LIKE TO TALK ABOUT AT TRADE SHOWS AND CONFERENCES

- New products and trends
- Changes in industry regulations
- Upcoming industry shows
- Product demonstrations
- Personnel and management changes
- Customer incentive programs

- Travel stories
- Local restaurants and entertainment

CONVERSATION TIP FOR
ALL NETWORKING STYLES

Demonstrating Credibility

People use *direct statements* when they want to leave little doubt as to their desired meaning and clearly want to express their opinions, positions, or what they want others to do.

People use *implied statements* if they are oversensitive to disapproval or if they are unsure about how others may react or feel about a topic, opinion, position, or course of action. While implied statements may be less opinionated or confrontational than direct statements, they are more likely to create misunderstandings and incorrect assumptions.

Competitive and **Analytical Networkers** can come across as blunt or confrontational if they make direct statements with their arms folded and a stern look on their face. Unfolding your arms and smiling as you say what you mean will suggest strength and confidence without sounding harsh.

Outgoing and **Amiable Networkers** can sound weak or, in extreme cases, evasive if they use too many implied statements. For more credibility and impact, make an effort to communicate to clarify rather than to mollify.

OPENING LINES AT TRADE SHOWS
AND CONFERENCES

To a Trade Show or Conference Manager

> "What's the biggest challenge in putting together a trade show like this?"
>
> "What would you say are the biggest mistakes vendors make when attending trade shows?"
>
> "What would you suggest our staff do to get the most from this trade show?"
>
> "I have ideas for new trade show marketing programs, but I lack funds. Any suggestions?"

To a Rep or Sales Manager Working in a Vendor Booth

> "What have you found to be your most popular product with people attending the show?"
>
> "Tell me a little more about your customers so when I meet one I can tell them about you."
>
> "How do you usually follow up with the prospects you meet at the show?"

To a Potential Customer in a Trade Show or Conference Booth

> "Please tell me a little about what brings you to this trade show (conference)."
>
> "What is the most useful kind of information I can give you?"
>
> "What do you think of our company's new line of products?"
>
> "What other new products do you think you'd be interested in looking at?"

> ### ⊘ Taboo Topics at Trade Shows and Conferences ⊘
>
> ✗ competitors' poor products or track record
> ✗ unfriendly competitors ✗ unpleasant experiences
> with competitors ✗ troublesome clients or competitors
> ✗ fraudulent business practices ✗ talking too
> much about products or services ✗ excessive
> "extracurricular" activities

MAKE TRADE SHOWS AND CONVENTIONS PAY OFF FOR OTHERS, TOO

In this chapter you've learned that networkers at trade shows and conventions are open to just about any conversation that may lead to business opportunities. That's why positioning yourself as a resource and emphasizing how you can help others achieve their business goals will increase your contacts, your referrals, and your profits.

16

Workshops

If you are like many motivated businesspeople these days, you attend professional development workshops. Workshops provide golden opportunities for networking for several reasons. Most people attending workshops enjoy meeting and talking to other like-minded individuals who also strive to upgrade their skills and goals. Plus, many are not shy about demonstrating their abilities and telling others about their accomplishments. After sharing your immediate workshop objectives—that is, what you want to learn in the class—it is easy to extend the conversation to other common interests and mutually beneficial business topics. The sooner you discover areas of commonality, levels of expertise, and business goals, the faster you can develop the business relationship.

If you attend an interactive workshop, then you have the opportunity to participate with other attendees in paired, group, and full class activities. Once attendees see how others perform in class exercises, you are in a great position to fulfill two more networking goals—demonstrating your approach to problem-solving and assessing how you might help others, either directly or indirectly through referrals. Never begin your relationship other attendees in a workshop by trying to sell them your products or services. Instead, position yourself as someone who will refer them customers or get them the help and resources they need to fulfill their business goals.

SOCIAL NETWORKING AND ONLINE LEARNING

If you want to expand your live workshop and business possibilities beyond the walls of the traditional classroom, training facility, or conference breakout session, then offer your programs online through client social networking sites. Although in-person and online learning goals are often the same, they have different challenges, drawbacks, and benefits. Social networking tools can help mitigate some drawbacks while maximizing benefits of online learning. For example, school or corporate social networks allow members to blog, see speaker profiles, learn about upcoming programs, provide feedback, update and access course materials, and find resources. And of course, networking opportunities with speakers and attendees via e-mail and instant messaging are just a click away.

Since online teaching and learning have moved from an emphasis on Web content to a more interactive format, speakers and attendees need to be technically competent, understand how to use social networking tools, and know how to facilitate interactions if they are to be successful online. According to online learning experts, if online learning is to be successful speakers must shift from "providers of knowledge" to "facilitators of knowledge" and attendees must go from being passive to active learners. Social networking sites and tools play a critical role in achieving these goals.

> To find more about workshops in your area, type: *social networks* + *(topic-related) workshops* into your favorite search engine.

TOPICS THAT MOST NETWORKERS LIKE TO TALK ABOUT AT WORKSHOPS AND CONFERENCES

- Business goals and interests
- Opinions of speakers at workshops
- Workshop objectives
- Related conferences
- Work responsibilities
- Interests outside of work
- Work-related issues
- History with their company

OPENING LINES AT WORKSHOPS AND CONFERENCES

Workshop Goals and Related Workshops

"What are you hoping to learn in today's workshop?"
"What is the most useful thing you've learned so far in the workshop?"

CONVERSATION TIP

Find a Workshop Buddy

Finding a workshop buddy with whom you share tasks, exercises, role playing, and other learning activities allows you to get to know each other fast. Many business relationships that begin in workshops continue long after the program is over.

"What are you hoping to get out of this course?"
"What other workshops have you attended?"
"This is my first time here. What about you?"
"Have you met some interesting people here?"
"What do you like best about the workshop so far?"

Personal Interests

"I enjoy other workshops in the area of . . . ."
"What do you enjoy doing when you're not working?"
"Do you have time to get a quick bite to eat after we finish the workshop?"

Business Interests

"What part of the business are you in that brings you to a workshop like this?"
"That was an interesting question you asked about . . . . That is what I do for my company."
"I know a vendor who would love to talk to you about your business. Do you want her contact information?"

🚫 TABOO TOPICS AT WORKSHOPS 🚫

✗ negative or crass comments about the workshop speaker ✗ complaints about your supervisor or company ✗ openly discussing changing companies ✗ negative comparisons of your company and another company ✗ complaints about other people attending the workshop ✗ upstaging the speaker ✗ conversations that interfere with the speaker or instruction ✗ group discussions outside the scope of the workshop ✗ monopolizing a Q&A session ✗ showing off your knowledge

WORKSHOPS ARE IDEAL SITUATIONS TO SPAWN BIG DEALS

You learned in this chapter that the sooner you establish contact with other workshop attendees, the more opportunities you'll have to network and explore mutual business interests. Learning about needs and abilities of others, uncovering your common interests, and seeing how you interact with others make workshops one of the best places to network for big deals.

17

Association Meetings

According to the Directory of Associations, published by the Concept Marketing Group, there are over 40,000 professional, business, and trade associations in the United States. Strategic networking at monthly association meetings is one of the best places to meet the leaders of your industry, learn about trends, mix with competitors, and prospect for business. Attending association meetings on a regular basis gives you the opportunity to initiate and build relationships with colleagues, customers, and competitors over time. If you become involved in your association, more people will know about you and what you do. As you share and promote your vision for the organization, your status and credibility as an industry leader will soar even higher.

Most association members will eagerly help meeting attendees learn about the benefits of membership and encourage them to join their organization. Nonmembers attend these meetings to gain industry information, make contacts, and consider membership. Both members and nonmembers will get better results networking if they focus their conversations around the meeting agenda and exchange information about each other's business, background, goals, and perception of industry trends.

USING SOCIAL NETWORKING TOOLS TO INCREASE ASSOCIATION MEMBERSHIP AND VALUE

Large or small, every association must grow its membership and provide value to remain healthy and vibrant, and now with the help of social networking tools this task has become easier—and a lot more fun! Social networking sites that customize their tools for associations offer members many ways in which they can promote their organization and programs, deliver information, facilitate member involvement, and deliver resources. Through social networking tools such as blogs and forums, members can communicate beyond the regular meetings, exchange information, get program feedback, develop better programs, share best practices, and create a community of colleagues to increase interest, create value, and encourage participation from their current and potential members.

To find more about associations near you, type: *association membership + social networking* into your favorite search engine.

TOPICS THAT MOST NETWORKERS LIKE TO TALK ABOUT AT ASSOCIATION MEETINGS

- Association marketing, sales, and promotion initiatives
- Industry trends and members in the news

- Association and industry leaders
- Internet and business technology
- Upcoming association programs
- Membership benefits
- Members' products and services
- Related organizations and awards
- Members' businesses and customers
- Association community projects
- Business goals related to the association

CONVERSATION TIP

Chatting with Competitors

Present a friendly competitor image by avoiding any direct confrontation or challenge. Keep your conversation light and professional by saying something like, "How are things with you these days?" Or "What do you think of the changes going on in our industry?"

OPENING LINES AT AN ASSOCIATION MEETING

To a Member of the Association

"What are some of your upcoming programs?"
"What are your association's goals over the next year?"
"How has being a member helped your business?"
"What does this association do for the community?"
"Who are the members of your association?"
"Who do I contact about becoming a member?"

To a Prospective Association Member

> "How did you find out about our association?"
>
> "I'm curious, what are you hoping to get from an organization like ours?"
>
> "Tell me a little about your business and I'll tell you how our organization can help you."

To a Fellow Attendee

> "What brought you to this association meeting?"
>
> "What part of this business are you in?"
>
> "I'm involved in a project related to this association."

TAKE THE OPPORTUNITY TO SPEAK OFF THE CUFF AT ASSOCIATION MEETINGS

In addition to raising your profile and image, impromptu speaking at an association meeting demonstrates your expertise, confidence, and speaking style. And it's no secret that most clients like to hire the people in the industry with the highest image and best reputation. By far, the most common mistake networkers make when speaking off the cuff is that they take too long to get to the point.

Here are a few additional speaking dos and don'ts for each networking style:

Competitive Networkers

☑ Do stress the benefits to your audience.

☒ Don't self-promote or boast.

Outgoing Networkers

☑ Do make your point right away.

☒ Don't talk too much.

Amiable Networkers

☑ Do look directly into the audience.
☒ Don't make vague statements.

Analytical Networkers

☑ Do state your conclusion first and simplify your explanation.
☒ Don't speak longer than your allotted time.

Here are various situations in which the four networking styles prefer to make off-the-cuff presentations:

- Competitive Networkers love to offer their opinions on any issue or topic.
- Amiable and Analytical Networkers prefer to present their views on topics or issues in which they are knowledgeable.
- Outgoing Networkers love to open ideas up to a group for discussion.
- Competitive and Outgoing Networkers enjoy pitching an upcoming event.
- Amiable and Analytical Networkers are usually happy to explain procedures.
- Outgoing Networkers make excellent appeals for volunteers.
- Competitive and Outgoing Networkers are the best ones to discuss industry trends.
- Competitive Networkers gladly present updated sales figures.
- Outgoing Networkers will be flattered to offer congratulations or propose a toast.

$\bigcirc$ **Taboo Topics at Association Meetings** $\bigcirc$

✗ ineffective association leadership ✗ poorly organized meetings ✗ troublesome members ✗ amateur speakers ✗ shoddy facilities ✗ association gossip and politics ✗ unappreciative members ✗ mediocre food ✗ hard-selling your products or services ✗ criticizing other associations

---

NETWORKING AT YOUR CUSTOMERS' ASSOCIATION MEETINGS FOCUSES YOUR MARKETING EFFORTS

In this chapter you learned small talk topics that easily segue into business discussions with other professionals at association meetings. In addition, when you incorporate your customers' association events into your overall networking strategy, you'll focus your efforts on making big deals in industries that can most benefit from your products and services.

Business Card Exchanges

What is one business event that nearly every city or town in the United States has in common? Chambers of Commerce, Rotary Clubs, civic groups, alumni associations, banks, for-profit and not-for-profit networking groups frequently sponsor business card exchanges. These organizations most often host breakfast meetings between 7 and 9 a.m. or after-hours events between 6 and 8 p.m. The crowds range from 25 to 250 people depending on the time of day, cost, and whether they are serving food and beverages.

Business card exchanges are a good opportunity to meet face-to-face with small business owners, association officers and members, industry and community leaders, some of your competitors, and representatives or executives from larger companies who frequently sponsor events for civic groups and small businesses.

If you make a presentation or purchase a vendor table at a business card exchange, it is a great opportunity to market your business's products or services, develop a network of contacts, and introduce your products and services to hundreds of potential customers.

SOCIAL NETWORKING FOR BUSINESS OWNERS AND ENTREPRENEURS

If you are a business owner, an entrepreneur, or are considering a business venture, visiting your local Chamber of Commerce Web site is a great place to begin making the connections you'll need to build your business. Long considered a gateway into the business community, Chamber of Commerce sites allow members to connect to a network of talented people, small business owners, and independent professionals in your community. Many offer online programs, calendars of events, announcements, forums, and blogs to share experiences, ask questions, seek advice, share leads, and give support.

Since the primary mission of a Chamber of Commerce is to promote local development and economic growth, many chambers offer "meet and greet" luncheons, workshops on the essentials of starting a business, or other events targeted at specific or niche groups with the goal of providing professional development, mentoring, and networking opportunities. Some of these special services or programs can include member listings, referrals, sales leads groups, executive exchange groups, "green" business forums, and retail cluster groups.

To find out about business card exchanges near you, type: *(your city)* + *Chamber of Commerce* + *business card exchange* + *social networking* into your favorite search engine.

TOPICS THAT MOST NETWORKERS LIKE TO TALK ABOUT AT BUSINESS CARD EXCHANGES

- Entrepreneurs and new businesses
- Personal business goals, promotions, and customer successes
- Local city politics (with care)
- Local business development initiatives
- Real estate
- Local business associations
- Community programs and events
- Local school and professional sports teams

OPENING LINES AT BUSINESS CARD EXCHANGES

Entrepreneurs and New Businesses

"What got you into your business?"

"What aspect of attending these exchanges do you find most helpful to your business?"

"What would you say your customers want most from you and your business?"

CONVERSATION TIP

Exchanging Business Cards

The next time someone hands you a business card, don't just stuff it in your pocket. Instead, take a few extra seconds to absorb the information, smile, nod your head in approval, and ask a question about something on the card. This is also the perfect time to silently restate the person's name to help you recall it later.

Community Programs and Events

> "I'd love to hear about some of your recent community programs."
> "What has been your biggest challenge as a community leader?"
> "What events are you planning for this year?"

Local Business Development Initiatives

> "How has the small business development program worked for your company?"
> "How would you suggest that I get a grant for my business?"

Real Estate

> "How has the recent change in real estate values affected your business?"
> "Do you happen to know of any available office space in the downtown area?"

Local Business Associations

> "I belong to several local business association. What about you?"

School, College, and Professional Sports Teams

> "Since our company is a sponsor for high school, college, and local sports teams, we like to go to the games."

Here are a few additional dos and don'ts for each networking style when attending a business card exchange:

Competitive Networkers

☑ Do demonstrate your leadership skills by offering to make a presentation at a future event.

☒ Don't make snap decisions about the people you meet.

Outgoing Networkers

☑ Do keep your conversations business oriented.

☒ Don't be overly optimistic about your business prospects.

Amiable Networkers

☑ Do set a realistic goal of introducing yourself to a specific number of people at the business card exchange.

☒ Don't be pressured into agreeing with another's point of view.

Analytical Networkers

☑ Do demonstrate that you can discuss a variety of subjects, in addition to business and your area of expertise.

☒ Don't overlook the "human element" when discussing technical issues.

⊘ Taboo Topics at Business Card Exchanges ⊘

✗ emotionally charged politics ✗ local scandals ✗ unfriendly competitors ✗ unsuccessful city initiatives ✗ unpopular school coaches, principals, or teachers ✗ personal disputes ✗ unpopular city politicians

BIG-DEAL OPPORTUNITIES EMERGE THROUGH BUSINESS CARD EXCHANGES

You've learned in this chapter many common topics at business card exchanges that allow you to transition from small talk to community-related business projects. By tapping into a vast network of businesses that service the public and private sectors where you live, you'll be in a better position to meet government officials, get referrals, and capitalize on emerging business opportunities.

19

Lunch and Dinner Business Meetings

According to a quip by economist John Kenneth Galbraith, "In the United States all business not transacted over the telephone is accomplished in conjunction with alcohol or food, often under conditions of advanced intoxication." I suppose that's why so many people prefer discussing business over lunch or dinner. Chatting before, during, and after a business lunch or dinner with a client or prospect provides an opportunity for you to conduct business, soft sell, informally talk about a variety of topics, get to know one another and, of course, network. The challenge here is what to do first—get right down to business, warm up with small talk about a local sports team, or discuss mutually beneficial contacts. Since it's best to defer to your guest's conversational preferences in this situation, try to get a sense which he or she prefers: getting the "business out of the way" first and then enjoy eating and chatting about other topics or vice versa.

Be aware that to some clients, introducing a business or networking topic into the conversation before the meal arrives may seem pushy or crass. However, if you wait until the waiter brings you dessert or coffee, it may leave you with too little time to discuss the issues you hoped to explore. Since lunch usually offers you less time, consider discussing business right away, and then, as time permits, bring up networking topics before you finish the meal and the waiter brings coffee or dessert. With dinner, you generally have more time as you wait for the meal to arrive so you can make small talk or, if you and your guest prefer, discuss any specific business issues. Then as the evening wears on and the main business topics are out of the way, you can talk about other business-related issues or general topics related to your networking goals. If you are not sure where to start, you can simply ask your dining companion, "Would you prefer to discuss business now or after we eat?"

USE SOCIAL NETWORKING TO
CHOOSE THE RIGHT RESTAURANT

Your choice of a restaurant for an important client lunch or dinner says a lot about you and your approach to business and can make a big difference in the future of your relationship. Using social networking tools is a fast and reliable way to find up-to-date restaurant reviews. To avoid any embarrassment for you or your client, don't make reservations without first asking if he or she has any particular food preferences or restrictions. I guarantee that asking a steak lover to dine at a vegetarian restaurant or vice versa will not win you points.

You can cut through the sheer volume of restaurant choices by going to online blogs, forums, or Web sites. Then, even if you know the restaurant, check out their

Web site for the recent reviews, the latest menu, seating arrangement, lighting, noise level, and prices.

To find out more about the best places for a business lunch or dinner, type: *(your city)* + *(preferred cuisine)* + *restaurant reviews* into your favorite search engine.

TOPICS THAT MOST NETWORKERS LIKE TO TALK ABOUT AT LUNCH OR BUSINESS MEETINGS

- Company staffing and training
- New marketing and sales initiatives
- Changing industry climate
- Challenges from competitors
- Five-year plan for business growth
- Favorite charities or company projects
- Golf game/professional sports
- Family life and home renovation
- Special projects or hobbies

CONVERSATION TIP FOR ALL NETWORKING STYLES
Revealing Background Information

Successful networkers exchange some background information to quickly establish rapport, commonality, and to determine the potential for further professional or social contact. By adapting your approach to each individual you can make the person feel more comfortable talking to you. Be sure to balance the exchange of information, but do not seek or divulge sensitive or overly personal background information until you know the individual better.

Competitive Networkers prefer to ask and answer background questions that focus on status, action, results, and goals. **Tip:** Take care not to be overly aggressive, inflate your accomplishments, or denigrate the accomplishments of others.

Outgoing Networkers prefer to ask and answer background questions that allow for an abundance of feelings, experiences, and details. **Tip:** Pay special attention to balancing the exchange of information.

Amiable Networkers prefer to ask and answer background questions that allow the conversation to remain somewhat neutral. **Tip:** Be a bit more assertive by asking for and revealing enough specific information to encourage deeper follow-up questions and additional self-disclosures.

Analytical Networkers often prefer to ask and answer closed-ended background questions that focus on facts and solving problems. **Tip:** Avoid comparing résumés or questioning the credibility of others' achievements.

OPENING LINES AT A LUNCH OR BUSINESS MEETING

To a Client or Prospect Who Prefers to Talk Business First

> "Is it okay if we first order our meal and then get right down to business?"
>
> "I'd like to discuss an idea I had that I think can help you increase your business."

To a Client or Prospect Who Prefers to Chat Informally Before Discussing Business

> "Before we get down to business, how was your weekend?"

"I understand that we both support the same charity. What's got you involved?"

To a Client or Prospect in Human Resources, Training, or Sales

"What made you decide to go into the human resources side of the business?"

"In a perfect world where money and time are not an issue, what kind of training program would you offer employees of your company?"

"What do you see as the major obstacle for your reps reaching their sales goals?"

To a Guest Who Sits Quietly Waiting for You to Open the Conversation

"This restaurant's menu is quite interesting. What looks good to you?"

"What would you like to discuss?"

"I'd like to tell you about a project that I hope you will find interesting enough to become involved in."

⃠ TABOO TOPICS IN LUNCH AND DINNER BUSINESS MEETINGS ⃠

✗ food poisoning ✗ medical problems or issues
✗ gory crimes ✗ distasteful stories ✗ restaurant horror stories ✗ unappetizing descriptions of how food products are produced ✗ grousing about other clients
✗ complaining about the economy or business
✗ health problems or personal issues

DINING YOUR WAY TO BIG DEALS

In this chapter you learned that it's best to adapt your preference of when to bring up a business topic at a meal to that of the person with whom you are dining. Given that you only have a limited time to talk over a meal, open with small topics that easily segue into the main business issues so you can focus your conversation on potential big deals.

20

Corporate Cafeterias

You don't have to wait for an industry conference or association meeting to network when your company's cafeteria is crowded with lunchtime diners every day, many of whom may know about opportunities in their departments, with associates, vendors, or other employers. With daily opportunities to chat over a sandwich or bowl of soup, there's no reason you can't use some of that time to network in your company's cafeteria and explore mutual opportunities—plus you'll never have to eat lunch alone.

Make a point of eating in the cafeteria on a regular basis and more or less at the same time so you can see who else takes lunch when you do. Look around and see who looks friendly and open for contact. Then take a seat at a nearby table, make eye contact, and smile. If the person returns your smile and eye contact, then take the risk and offer a casual greeting to break the ice and get the conversation going.

SOCIAL NETWORKING FOR THE LUNCH BUNCH

If you want to do some networking at lunch, then join a growing number of people in your area who have the same idea. These folks are part of a social networking phenomenon called Lunch 2.0. It all started in Silicon Valley when Web 2.0 employees met up for lunch and migrated from one corporate cafeteria to another to meet, eat (sometimes free food), and chat. While these get-togethers were not specifically designated as networking events, people shared job opportunities, industry news, and the latest and greatest electronic gadgets.

As they increase in popularity, Lunch 2.0 and other social networking sites that offer announcements of lunch meetings based on specific interests are more often held in local restaurants. They tend to be loosely organized and as focused on the food as on the topic or unifying interest of the group.

To find out more about "lunch clubs" in corporate cafeterias near you, type: *(your city)* + *Lunch 2.0* + *social networking* into your favorite search engine.

TOPICS THAT MOST NETWORKERS LIKE TO TALK ABOUT IN CORPORATE CAFETERIAS

- Today's lunch/favorites on the menu
- New focus on healthy menu choices
- Restaurants outside the cafeteria
- Departments where you work
- Job descriptions and current projects
- Past employment

- Corporate news
- Where people live/how they get to work
- Corporate sponsored programs, workshops and volunteer projects
- Stores in the immediate neighborhood
- Employment opportunities within the company
- Mutual friends, acquaintances, and family
- Interests outside of work
- Career goals

OPENING LINES IN THE CORPORATE CAFETERIA

Favorites on the Menu/Outside Restaurants

"That looks good! What's for lunch today?"
"What are some of your favorite things to eat here?"
"What do you think of the cafeteria's healthy choices menu?"

Job Descriptions, Current Projects, Past Employment

"Hi, my name's . . . . I work in the . . . department."
"What projects are you working on these days?"

CONVERSATION TIP

No Grousing at Lunch

If you've had a rough morning, it's natural to blow off some steam at lunch with a coworker. However, avoid making job or personal complaints regular lunchtime topics of conversation or you may soon find yourself eating lunch alone.

"One of the things I really like about my job is . . . ."
"What other kinds of work have you done?"
"What did you like best about working at . . . ?"

Company News/Sponsored Programs

"Here's what I think about the new . . . that our company
is planning."
"I attended an interesting lunchtime workshop last week
that showed how to . . . ."

Interests Outside of Work

"What kinds of things do you enjoy doing when you're not
working?"
"Did you do anything fun this weekend?"
"I'm a food lover. That's why I like to explore new restaurants in my spare time."
"Let me know if you'd like to join me sometime for a bite
to eat after work."

Job Opportunities

"Any openings in your department?"
"What's the management team like in your department?"
"What are the chances of me getting a shot at an available
position in your department?"
"What would you suggest I do to get an interview with one
of the managers in your department?"

Here are a few more tips based on networking styles for
making small talk in the company cafeteria:

Competitive Networkers. When discussing sports, politics, or any other hot button topics in the cafeteria, don't get into debates. Remember that the purpose of your conversation is to build rapport with coworkers, not to persuade them.

Outgoing Networkers. Instead of just chatting with your immediate coworkers at lunch, introduce yourself to someone from another department and strike up a conversation about something work-related.

Amiable Networkers. Rather than reading a newspaper or book between bites in the cafeteria at lunch, sit nearby a person you'd like to meet. Break the ice with an easy-to-answer question or compliment about his or her lunch. If you get a friendly response, introduce yourself, and exchange information about your jobs.

Analytical Networkers. Instead of sitting alone and using your cell phone, playing a video game, or listening to your iPod, take a seat near someone with a friendly face. Smile, make eye contact, and then offer a positive comment or ask an easy-to-answer question about work, the food, or something occurring in your immediate environment.

$\bigcirc$ Taboo Topics in Corporate Cafeterias $\bigcirc$

✗ gossip about coworkers or supervisors ✗ confidential job plans ✗ confidential corporate information ✗ misappropriation of company funds or property ✗ managerial incompetence ✗ food preparation horror stories ✗ complaints about the food ✗ pushing too hard for a job reference

FROM LITTLE MEALS TO BIG DEALS

You've learned in this chapter that making small talk in the corporate cafeteria is as much about building relationships with people you see every day as it is about qualifying prospects. Breaking the ice with "So what are you having for lunch today?" to chatting about a variety of business-related topics provides you with frequent opportunities to help each other achieve your networking goals and uncover potential big deals.

21

Department Meetings

Meetings! Meetings! Meetings! Although sometimes you may wonder what gets done, departmental meetings present great opportunities to find out what on-the-job challenges and issues coworkers, supervisors, and managers face. Savvy networkers see these problems as an opportunity to position themselves as a resource to either directly come up with solutions or by finding others who can assist in solving the problems. This is what strategic networking is all about! However, if you make some small talk with a few people before the meeting begins, it can help lead you to a big deal by better determining their particular needs, desired outcomes, sense of urgency, communication style, and what insights or suggestions from you that they may appreciate or find the most helpful.

Actively participate in departmental meetings by asking both closed- and open-ended questions. Your closed-ended, short answer questions, such as "What exactly are the specs?" "When is the deadline?" and "What do you need from me to get started?" demonstrate your ability to focus on details so that the job gets done right, the first time! Your open-ended and broader range questions, such as "What do you see happening as a result of this project?" "How do you see the situation as it stands now and how do you want it to change?" and "What would a successful outcome look like?" show a desire to see the "big picture" and understand the long-term goals and objectives of your department and company.

Your overall involvement in the discussion shows an interest in your department's project and that you want to help your boss succeed and look good to his or her superiors.

Take care how you respond to the suggestions of others at a departmental meeting, particularly if they come from your boss or peers. If you are participating in brainstorming sessions keep any negative opinions to yourself, since the idea behind brainstorming is to first get all the ideas on the table—then consider their merits afterward. If you do disagree with an idea, have a criticism or better idea, you should consider offering your point of view only as an opinion, not a fact. But beware, being overly critical will not win you any friends on the job. Plus, avoid side conversations with coworkers during departmental meetings not only because they are distracting, but also because they can imply your disapproval or a lack of enthusiasm for what was said and the person who spoke.

TAPPING INTO YOUR CORPORATE SOCIAL NETWORK

Do you work in an organization and want to find a job in a different part of the company? Are you looking to fill positions in your department, but prefer to recruit new staff from within your organization? Is your team or business situated in different locations, but the individuals need to be linked so they can quickly exchange information, feedback, and ideas? Do you want to leverage your relationships with past employees who have gone to work for your clients?

The mission of an organization's corporate social networking site is to help its members reinforce or reestablish old relationships and create new contacts within their enterprise. They accomplish this by continuing personal connections among and between groups of employees, former colleagues, alumni, and others to increase knowledge sharing and productivity. Corporate social networking sites offer their members blogs, forums, job postings, applications, mentoring, referrals, and other ways to initiate and maintain contact within their organization and industry. If you want to boost productivity, retain staff, increase new business, and rehire old employees, then tap into your corporate social network.

To learn more about your company or organization's social network, type: *(your company or organization)* + *social network* into your favorite search engine.

TOPICS THAT MOST NETWORKERS LIKE TO TALK ABOUT AT DEPARTMENTAL MEETINGS

- Department projects
- Department staffing and training
- Interdepartmental communication
- New software programs and training
- Upcoming and recent vacations
- Industry news and personnel changes
- New products
- Sales and marketing ideas
- Management changes
- Mutual acquaintances

OPENING LINES AT DEPARTMENTAL MEETINGS

Department Projects

> "What's the most challenging part of your project?"
> "What can I do to help you complete the project?"
> "Which part of the new upcoming project do you want to work on?"

Department Staffing and Training

> "How do you see our staffing needs changing over the next six months or so?"
> "What recommendations would you suggest in terms of our staffing for this next project?"
> "What are some of the things you'd like to do with the new software, but don't know how to do?"
> "What kind of training would be most helpful to you?"

CONVERSATION TIP

Building Rapport in Person

If you communicate with coworkers mostly via e-mail, the department meeting may be the only time you have an opportunity to meet face-to-face. Spending a few minutes to chat before or after the meeting can build rapport and make coworkers feel you are friendly and open to contact.

Interdepartmental Communication

> "In your view, what are the most important topics to cover at the next meeting?"

"What do you think we can do to improve how we communicate with one another?"

Mutual Acquaintances

"Have you heard recently from our friend, . . . ?"

"Your name came up when I was chatting with an ex coworker at our association meeting."

"Who else at that company have you worked with?"

Family News, Upcoming and Recent Vacations

"Before we start with our meeting, how was your vacation?"

"I'd like to hear more about your wedding plans."

"How do you balance work and family?"

Industry News and Personnel Changes

"What kind of person do like working with?"

"Who is the new person joining our department?"

"I heard about the new regulations. How do you think they will affect us?"

New Products

"Of all the things we sell, what's your favorite?"

"So tell me what you think of our new . . . ?"

"I think that was a great idea you brought up at last week's meeting on new product development. How did you come up with that?"

New Sales and Marketing Programs

> "I think I know what customers look for when they con-
> sider a new product."
> "Can you give me an example of how are we planning to
> market this new product?"
> "I like your marketing plan. What do you suggest we
> do next?"

Here are a few more conversation tips based on networking styles for speaking at department meetings:

Competitive Networkers. Converse with your coworkers, don't
compete.

Outgoing Networkers. Pay attention and contribute. Avoid side
conversations or crass comments.

Amiable Networkers. Don't be timid about offering your ideas
and suggestions.

Analytical Networkers. Listen for and contribute to desired outcomes instead of pointing out the minor mistakes of others.

🚫 TABOO TOPICS IN DEPARTMENT MEETINGS 🚫

✗ spreading office gossip about new staff or personnel
changes ✗ criticizing ideas from brainstorming sessions
✗ anticipating negative results about upcoming projects
✗ showing no interest in topics outside of business
✗ not participating during brainstorming sessions
✗ not offering to help or make any contacts for those
who need assistance ✗ sighing, moaning, or rolling your
eyes when someone says something that you disagree with

MAKING SMALL TALK AT DEPARTMENTAL MEETINGS ALLOWS YOU TO SHARPEN YOUR PITCH

In this chapter you learned that it's a valuable networking strategy to start conversations with your colleagues before meetings begin. Whether you chat with your boss, coworkers, subordinates, or clients about upcoming vacations, kids, or specific business issues, by engaging you can immediately assess their comfort levels, communication styles, and even answer questions that can increase their receptivity when you discuss ideas or pitch a big deal.

22

Office Elevators

"**G**oing up?" The next time you take your daily 30-second ride in an elevator full of coworkers and clients, instead of silently staring at the electronic display as you pass floors, why not engage some of your colleagues in conversation? True, you may have a limited amount of time to talk, but if you share with others your brief ride on a daily basis, you can initiate contact with the knowledge that you probably will see them again sometime soon or at the same time the next day. By taking the opportunity to break the ice and make small talk, albeit brief, you are sending a signal that you are friendly, confident, and open for contact.

Where a short conversation in an elevator at work can lead to depends on the person with whom you're talking. For example, if you take the initiative to engage a high-ranking company executive in the elevator, then he or she will probably see you as a confident and outgoing worker. Needless to say that's a good first impression that can pay off at a later date, especially if your name comes up regarding a job promotion or other opportunity for you within the company. Or, if you break the ice and offer assistance to a client on his or her way to a meeting, then you're sending the signal that you and your company want to connect with the customers you serve. Again, you have made a positive impression in a brief time on an influential person who you may at some point see again in a more formal capacity. Also, consider how good you can make a newcomer to your department feel by engaging the person in a brief conversation. Being friendly and willing to chat with a coworker even if it's for just 30 seconds can be the beginning of a great working relationship or even a friendship.

NEWS SOCIAL NETWORKS CAN FACILITATE YOUR ELEVATOR RIDE

Although many large buildings have installed small televisions in their elevators, even a short elevator ride can seem like an eternity when passengers stand side-by-side in silence. It's easy to break the ice in an elevator simply by referring to something you hear on the elevator TV. Then follow up your comment with a "self disclosure" such as "Oh, I just read about that online at my favorite news Web site (or some other news social networking site, of which there are many)!"

You don't have to be brilliant or offer any deep insights. After all, you've only got a few moments to chat, but your reference to a social networking that focuses on news will quickly give you and your elevator companion(s) something to talk about. Plus, by referring to a news-focused social network will give others the impression that you like to stay informed and get your news from up-to-the-minute sources.

> To find local news shows in your area, type: (your *favorite news organizations*) + *social networks* + (*your city*) into your favorite search engine.

TOPICS THAT MOST NETWORKERS LIKE TO TALK ABOUT IN ELEVATORS AT WORK

- Local places to eat or shop
- Company news or projects
- Places to walk during lunch
- Mutual friends or colleagues
- Cafeteria food recommendations
- Company employment opportunities
- Current department projects
- Which departments people work in

OPENING LINES IN OFFICE ELEVATORS

To a Company Executive or Manager

> "I read about your team's new product in our newsletter. How are the sales going so far?"

CONVERSATION TIP FOR ALL NETWORKING STYLES

Skip the Elevator Sales Pitch

Pitching yourself to others in an elevator can backfire. A better networking strategy is to say something that will make the other person smile and want to chat with you again later or on your next ride.

"Is that job posting for assistant manager in your department still open?"

To a Client

"Who are you working with these days?"
"Is after lunch a good time to discuss the new package designs?"

To a Coworker You Don't Know or a Newcomer to Your Office

"We work on the same floor, and I see you every day, but we've never formally met. I work in the . . . department. My name is . . . . What's yours?"
"Hello, are you new here? If you need anything, just ask. I sit in front of the sales office."

Here are a few more conversation tips based on networking styles for making small talk in elevators:

Competitive Networkers. Make friendly and light conversation —not aggressive "elevator" pitches.

Outgoing Networkers. When you talk to a person in the elevator, maintain a casual tone, but don't be overly familiar with someone you don't know.

Amiable Networkers and Analytical Networkers. Smile and make eye contact with others as you or they enter the elevator. Say hello and initiate small talk with someone who looks friendly or familiar.

⊘ Taboo Topics in Office Elevators ⊘

✗ power outages and people trapped in elevators
✗ office building fires ✗ terrorism ✗ corruption in the
building trades ✗ gossip about coworkers or clients
✗ job complaints ✗ private lives of coworkers
✗ confidential company information ✗ unannounced
mergers, layoffs, or personnel changes

ELEVATOR SMALL TALK CAN TAKE YOU TO THE TOP

In this chapter you learned that networking in elevators is about building instant rapport and not about giving a 30-second sales pitch to a trapped audience. Make your networking in elevators light, brief, and optional, based on the openness of your fellow passengers. When you get a friendly response from someone inside the elevator and if you exit on the same floor, continue your conversation after you leave the car. It could be the first stop on your way to a big deal.

23

Office Parties

Yahoo—it's party time! Networking at an office party with your peers can pay off with better working relationships and increased opportunities to move up in your company. However, if you are like a lot of people in today's large offices, you may not know many of the people who work on the same floor as you, only nod to those you pass in the hall, or silently ride in the elevator with them each day. Attending the holiday office party gives you permission to break through the invisible barrier that often separates people at work and say hello, start a conversation, discover mutual interests and, hopefully, help each other, either directly or indirectly, achieve your goals.

Holiday office parties with clients provide even greater opportunities for meeting new prospects and deepening existing relationships. During the holiday party you can sincerely express your gratitude for your client's business, chat about the future, and discuss business challenges and projects for the coming year. Capitalize on your client's holiday spirit and, if you truly have provided value to your client over the past year, consider asking for a referral, testimonial, or advice about a particular goal or activity you wish to pursue.

While holiday office parties have a huge potential for achieving your networking goals, bear in mind that they are *not* social events, but rather slightly less formal business functions that follow the basic rules of business etiquette. In other words, never do or say anything at a holiday office party that you wouldn't want your mother to know about or that you might have to apologize for the next day. In addition, although many people enjoy socializing at the holiday office party, most shy coworkers and clients generally dread having to attend this annual function and are often only there out of obligation. Plus, there are some people, for one reason or another, who simply do not enjoy the holiday season. To effectively network with these people, keep your conversation light and low key so you can put them at ease as quickly as possible.

MAKE SURE YOUR SOCIAL NETWORKING PROFILE IS PROFESSIONAL

"I saw your wild photos online. Wow, you really know how to party!" may sound like a compliment, but if those words come from your boss, a colleague, or a potential client, they more likely mean, "Forget about any hope of a promotion or sale." Social networking sites allow people an opportunity to get an idea of what others are like before they actually meet in person, so you want to make sure you are giving others with whom you work the right impression—and in business, that means "professional."

Therefore, before you head out the door for the next office party to mix and mingle, take a few minutes to check and update your online profiles, especially on the more popular social networking sites where you may have, in a moment of unbridled spontaneity, taken a few liberties with your words and photos. Delete any unprofessional pictures, comments, or language that may lead to embarrassing questions, misunderstandings, or unintended sentiments. If you are not sure what's appropriate or inappropriate online, follow this rule: "When in doubt—leave it out."

To find out the latest news related to your industry, type: *(your industry)* + *(your company)* + *social networking* into your favorite search engine.

TOPICS THAT MOST NETWORKERS LIKE TO TALK ABOUT AT OFFICE HOLIDAY PARTIES

- Vacation plans
- Personal goals, projects, resolutions
- Family reunions
- Holiday and religious celebrations
- Food, music, sports, and entertainment
- Recent past and future business projects
- Home renovations
- Unique gifts and charity

OPENING LINES AT HOLIDAY PARTIES

Recent Work Projects

"What was the most interesting project you worked on this year?"

"How do you see our project's success affecting next year's budget?"

CONVERSATION TIP

Office Party Etiquette

No matter what anyone tells you about letting your hair down and having fun, never do or say anything at a holiday office party that you wouldn't want your mother to read about in the newspaper the next morning.

"If you could have done anything differently with this project, what would it have been?"

Personal Goals and Projects

"Do you have any special projects planned for next year?"
"What made you decide to pursue that?"
"I've always wanted to learn how to . . . ."

Vacation Plans

"If you had all the time and money in the world, where would you go on vacation?"
"If you could recommend a place to go over the holidays, where would it be?"
"How do you celebrate the holidays?"
"What do you enjoy doing most while on vacation?

Conversational Bridges to Business Topics

"Are you interested in going to a 'start your own business' workshop with me?"
"Have you read any good business books lately?"
"I have a small decorating business. If you need help, I can give you a quote."

"I sell gifts for all occasions. If you're looking for a gift, here's my Web site address."

Here are a few reminders for each networking style when attending office parties:

Competitive Networkers. Use nonbusiness topics to break the ice and start conversations at office parties. Keep your conversation light and "shop talk" to a minimum.

Outgoing Networkers. Listen carefully to what coworkers and clients tell you at office parties regarding opportunities they seek and ones that are available. While you may discuss them briefly at the party, it's better to wait until you are sure you can talk privately.

Amiable Networkers. At the office party, introduce yourself to anyone new working in your office. Make newcomers feel welcome by introducing them to others who share your workspace or are on your team.

Analytical Networkers. Be ready to talk about several nontechnical topics that you feel comfortable with and think others will also enjoy talking about. You don't have to be an expert on the topic, a personal interest will do.

🚫 TABOO TOPICS IN OFFICE PARTIES 🚫

✗ gory crime ✗ war ✗ political corruption
✗ pollution ✗ poverty ✗ medical problems
✗ personal, money, family, job problems ✗ sad stories
✗ office gossip ✗ poor management decisions
✗ past overindulgences ✗ hard-selling your
side business products or services

NETWORKING AT OFFICE PARTIES KEEPS YOU
IN THE OPPORTUNITY LOOP

In this chapter you learned that networking at office parties can uncover opportunities inside your company. You now know what small-talk topics can help zero in on the business and professional interests that you share with fellow coworkers. Once you make this transition, the next toast you'll be making at the office party might be about a future big deal.

PART IV

SOCIAL SITUATIONS: OPENING LINES, TOPICS, AND NETWORKING STRATEGIES

24

Four Rules of Networking Etiquette in Social Situations

A social situation is one in which people meet with friends or associates for the purposes of having fun, seeking companionship, discussing common interests, and engaging in personal, physical, or spiritual pursuits. Social situations can provide excellent opportunities to turn small talk into big deals because people tend to be informal and chat about a wider range of topics, some of which may pertain to your work or business. Plus, you'll have an opportunity to meet businesspeople or possible clients who you may not normally come in contact with in your typical work-related situations. While some rules of networking etiquette in business and social situations overlap, there are some important differences.

In addition, if you are aware of the individual preferences of each networking style, including topics to bring up and subjects and phrases to use and avoid, you will be more successful while networking in social situations.

Competitive Networkers may be less comfortable in social situations if others prefer not to "talk shop" or discuss business. Phrases such as "I hate talking shop at parties" will turn off a Competitive Networker. You can bring up personal interests, hobbies, sports, or family, but avoid emotional topics or personal disclosures.

Outgoing Networkers are at their best in social situations, but may get their feelings hurt if you ignore them or consider their banter frivolous. Avoid phrases such as "Blah, blah, blah" or "Can't you be serious for a moment?" Outgoing Networkers will probably make fun of you if you try to bring up a serious topic in a social situation.

Amiable Networkers prefer social situations where they can talk one-on-one or in small groups with people they already know. Avoid surprise requests that put them on the spot in front of the group with phrases such as "How about singing us a song?" or "Tell everyone about the time you . . . ."

Analytical Networkers can feel uncomfortable in social situations where they don't know many of the other guests, so pushing them too hard to mingle may result in them prematurely leaving the party or activity. Once you find their areas of interest, they will open up, but avoid asking them too many technical questions or for advice, as you may hear more than you ever wanted to know.

The following networking rules of etiquette will help you connect the right way with the many different people you'll meet in social situations.

1. *Make small talk before networking for business.* Many people consider "shop talk" something to avoid in a social situation, particularly when in the initial stages of a conversation with a new acquaintance. Therefore,

begin your exchange with questions and comments
oriented around where you are situated and general
topics such as personal interests, hobbies, mutual
friends, vacations, or culture. Casually drop into your
conversation a few keywords or phrases about your
business or how you make your living. Then wait for
the other person to comment or ask you a question
before opening up business as a topic of discussion.

2. *Limit "shop talk" and business discussions in social sit-*
   uations. Discussing work-related and business issues
   in social situations offers many opportunities to
   uncover needs and explore possible future contact, so
   as business topics do arise, briefly discuss them. However, don't go on too long about your business, services, or experience, or you run the risk of boring others
   and leaving them out of the conversation. If someone
   does express a genuine interest in your business, then
   suggest pursuing the matter in more detail the following day on the telephone or in person.

3. *If a person clearly does not want to discuss business,*
   then change the topic. Although most people will tell
   you what they do for a living while chatting in a social
   situation, some simply may not want to talk business
   or discuss their work, and pressureing them will probably only cause them to dislike you. However, if a person mentions a problem or issue for which you can
   help, or he or she asks you more about your business,
   then you can assume that the topic is open to discussion, but proceed slowly.

4. *Don't reveal too much personal information too soon.*
   Building any relationship requires time and trust, and
   although most people are willing to disclose some personal information about themselves in social situa-

tions, revealing too much too soon can doom your relationship before it even has a chance to start. Revealing too much personal information suggests a lack of judgment and self-control. So, when you network at social events avoid bringing up or asking others about highly sensitive and personal topics.

FOLLOWING NETWORKING ETIQUETTE IN SOCIAL SITUATIONS CAN PAVE THE WAY TO PROFITS

In this chapter you learned that when networking in social situations you should not skip over small talk and dive directly into business topics; talk shop nonstop; open business discussions with those who prefer to talk about nonbusiness topics; or reveal too much personal information. When you follow these networking guidelines, the people you meet in social situations will ultimately be more open to conversations that center around potential business opportunities and big deals. Now you are ready to learn how to apply these principles to networking in common social situations.

25

Dinner Parties

Dinner parties are great opportunities to network and connect with several key people at once and to develop new relationships and deepen existing ones. Depending on the size of the group, your conversations will probably involve anywhere from two to eight people, so you need to be ready to quickly and effortlessly shift topics as the number of participants shifts. Your networking goals in these situations are to uncover common general and business interests or issues, get a better understanding of how each individual communicates, determine how he or she approaches problem-solving, and decide on how willing each individual is to discuss business during the evening.

It is best to begin your conversations with a compliment or question about your host, the food, mutual friends, the guests, and your immediate surroundings such as the art, music, table setting, flower arrangements, and other informal topics of conversation. The conversational tone in this social setting needs to be one of friendship, hospitality, warmth, appreciation, and good cheer. Absolutely no unpleasant topics or overly serious business discussions allowed—at least not before or while eating dinner!

So how do you know when it's appropriate to switch to a business topic? The answer is by listening. I'm always saving any business-related keywords I hear during small talk so I can refer to them to make a natural transition to a business topic. For example, after a short pause in the conversation, I'll say something like, "Do you mind if I ask you a business question related to something you said earlier?"

SOCIAL NETWORKS FOR PEOPLE WHO LIKE TO DINE, DISCUSS, AND MAKE NEW FRIENDS

Dinner clubs are social networks where singles and couples members dine out in small or large groups at local restaurants. They may be focused on a specific cuisine, location, or even price range. The singles-oriented dinner clubs organize dinners for small groups of an equal number of men and women. Some screen members, extend the invitations, and create seating arrangements based on members' common interests, age, and availability. In general, social networking dinner clubs are for culinary professionals and food lovers dedicated to discovering and exploring new restaurants. If members wish, they can post comments about their dining experience, network, and build relationships with other members online and in person.

To find out more about recommended places to dine near you and to connect with others interested in dining, type: *(your town) social networking dinner clubs + restaurant reviews* into your favorite search engine.

TOPICS THAT MOST NETWORKERS
LIKE TO TALK ABOUT
AT DINNER PARTIES

- Home renovation and gardens
- Golf, tennis, and recreational sports
- Family, friends, and pets
- Cooking and kitchen appliances
- Entertainment systems
- Cars, tools, computers, and Internet
- Past and future vacations
- Collectibles, furniture, and hobbies
- Local restaurants and places of interest
- Local pro teams and kids' sports
- New business and home projects
- Neighbors and schools

Here is a tip for each networking style when attending a dinner party:

Competitive Networkers. Ignore any controversial comments other guests might make about your products, business, or industry.

Outgoing Networkers. Don't tell long stories about people whom the other guests do not know.

Amiable Networkers. If during the meal a guest makes a reference to a business opportunity for you, thank them and then bring it up with him or her later in private.

Analytical Networkers. Keep an open mind to the opinions of others.

CONVERSATION TIP FOR ALL
NETWORKING STYLES

Sharing Your Opinions

The writer Oliver Wendell Holmes, Sr., wisely observed, "Those who ask your opinion really want your praise, and will be contented with nothing less." Your observations about the people and things at social and business events are natural opening lines that can—if presented in the right way—lead to networking opportunities. However, if you offer unsolicited criticism or focus your comments on the negative, other networkers will see you as someone who views the world (including them) in a negative way. It's a better networking strategy to follow Mr. Holmes's advice: Look for and praise what you observe as the positive in others.

OPENING LINES AT DINNER PARTIES

To the Other Guests

> "How do you know our host?"
>
> "Are you in the same business as our host?"
>
> "Do you have a favorite cuisine?"
>
> "I really recommend this appetizer!"
>
> "That bracelet you're wearing is beautiful! Where is it from?"
>
> "Do you live nearby or did you have to travel a ways to get here?"

To the Host

"The food is absolutely wonderful! Where did it come from?"

"I love your home, particularly the art (books, furniture, etc.)."

"I couldn't help but notice that unusual piece of furniture! There must be a story behind it!"

"I want to hear all about what you've been doing lately."

"Where did you meet all these interesting people?"

"I want to introduce you to my friend."

CONVERSATIONAL BRIDGES TO BUSINESS TOPICS

"I heard you mention earlier that you just started a new business. I'd love to hear about it."

"You mentioned that you were working late. What kind of work do you do?"

"What was the biggest challenge you ever faced in your business?"

"What advice would you give someone going into your business today?"

"What are the trends in your industry these days?"

⊘ TABOO TOPICS AT DINNER PARTIES ⊘

✗ medical problems ✗ family or marital problems
✗ money problems ✗ deceased family members
✗ unpleasant media stories ✗ politics ✗ complaints
about family, neighbors, mutual friends,
or acquaintances ✗ job problems ✗ confidential
company information ✗ business problems

NETWORK AT DINNER PARTIES TO BUILD TRUST

In this chapter you learned how to make small talk at dinner parties and naturally transition from nonbusiness to business topics. You now know that the primary networking goal in this situation is not to close a "big deal," but rather to build enough rapport and trust with others that if a business topic or opportunity arises, you'll feel comfortable taking the discussion a step further.

26

Colleges

According to the latest figures from the National Center for Education Statistics, nearly 7 million adults 25 years of age and over were enrolled in college programs. Whether you're completing your bachelor's or advanced degree, attending law school or taking continuing education classes at your local community college, institutions of higher learning are great places to meet business-minded people and broaden your network.

In addition to your classes, there are many other excellent places and opportunities to network and meet people. Joining clubs, volunteer groups, sports teams, and other activities gives you a chance to apply what you've learned in school, plus they are natural places to break the ice, start conversations, and find people with whom you share interests and, possibly, career goals. You certainly don't have to go into business with your college friends to benefit from your relationships. However, by learning about one another's goals and dreams, you can help one another succeed through networking and sharing the connections you make throughout your professional life.

SOCIAL NETWORKING AMONG YOUNG ADULTS

According to a recent survey conducted by the online market research company Anderson Analytics of nearly 1,000 young adults from U.S. colleges and universities and among 18 to 24-year-old active users of the world's most popular social network, Facebook.com, social networking sites like Facebook or MySpace are twice as popular among young women as young men. The survey goes on to say that young men are "far more likely" than young women to use business-oriented social networking sites. In addition, the survey shows that young adults frequent social networks that offer members access to humor and entertainment, sports, politics, news, electronic gear and gadgets, online buying and selling, and of course, dating and relationships.

To learn what's most popular among younger college students, type: *top social networks for college students* into your favorite search engine.

TOPICS THAT MOST NETWORKERS IN COLLEGE LIKE TO TALK ABOUT

- Career options and job market
- Current employment and work history
- Business, economics, and money
- Classes, professors, exams, and programs

- Fitness, health, and food
- Government, politics, and military
- People, media, and culture
- Law, medicine, religion, and ethics
- Family
- Pro sports and college teams
- Music, movies, TV, and pop culture
- Clubs and personal interests
- Internet Web sites and social networks
- Science, technology, and ecology
- Volunteer organizations
- Travel

Here are a few more networking tips for each networking style when attending a college class:

Competitive Networkers. Make it a point to consistently participate in small talk with other students before class, on breaks, or after class. Uncover and focus on the professional objectives of other students by asking them how a particular skill or issue fits into their overall business goals.

Outgoing Networkers. Make it a point to keep your small talk with other students focused on business-related topics by closely tying the class content to your own and their business objectives.

Amiable Networkers. Make it a point to consistently participate in small talk with other students before class, on breaks, or after class. Ask others how they have already or how they plan to use the class content regarding their business or career.

Analytical Networkers. Make it a point to participate in small talk with other students before class, on breaks, or after class. Prior to presenting your opinion on a particular business topic, paraphrase the ideas and positions of others to show you listen, understand, and consider issues from various points of view.

OPENING LINES IN COLLEGE

Career Options and Job Market

"What made you decide to attend this college?"
"How did you decide what area to major in?"
"If you could have your dream career, what would it be?"
"What are you planning to do after graduation?"

Current Employment and Work History

"I work at . . . . Do you have a job or are you looking for work?"
"Have you had any luck getting work through social networks?"
"I've always wanted to be in business for myself. Has that ever been an interest of yours?"
"What do you think is most important on your résumé?"

Classes, Professors, Exams, and Programs

"What made you decide on that major?"
"Tell me about one of your best classes."
"What do you like best about teaching?"
"Who has had the most influence on choosing your career?"

Clubs, Volunteer Groups, and Special Interests

"I belong to a club that you may find interesting. Do you want to come with me sometime and see what it's about?"

"What do you enjoy doing when you're not attending classes?"

"I volunteer twice a week at . . . ."

Fitness, Health, and Food

"What do you think is the best way to stay in shape?"

"I love good food. What places can you recommend that are nearby?"

"Would you be interested in joining me for a bite to eat after class sometime?"

CONVERSATIONAL BRIDGES TO BUSINESS TOPICS

"I have a friend who works at that company. Maybe she can help you meet the right person to get an interview. Do you want me to make a phone call for you?"

"My boss is looking for someone like you to . . . . Are you interested?"

"Can I run a business idea by you and see what you think?"

"I'm retiring from teaching soon and starting a new business."

⃠ TABOO TOPICS AT COLLEGE ⃠

✗ child abuse ✗ substance abuse ✗ mental illness
✗ suicide ✗ family crises ✗ spousal abuse ✗ abortion
✗ medical problems ✗ financial problems
✗ school problems ✗ legal problems

SMALL TALK AT COLLEGE BUILDS NETWORKING CONTACTS

You learned in this chapter that when you attend college courses and converse with students and instructors, your networking opportunities and contacts increase. You now know that by uncovering common goals and interests and then transitioning to related business topics, you will find others who share your goal of turning small talk into big deals.

27

Volunteer Groups

According to a recent press release by the Bureau of Labor Statistics of the U.S. Department of Labor, approximately 60 million people volunteered through or for an organization at least once within the past year. That makes the proportion of the population who volunteered at about 26 percent. You'll not only feel good about helping others, but volunteer groups are excellent environments in which to network because people who volunteer often hold positions of influence or have connections in other organizations that may need your products or services.

From a strategic networking perspective, which organizations should you volunteer for? The answer to that question depends on several factors, the most important of which is, are you passionate about the cause and willing to honor your commitment? Without passion and commitment, your efforts will come across as hollow and self-serving. Next, do your skills match the critical needs of the organization? Your value to the organization increases if you volunteer your highest and most unique set of professional skills. After all, any volunteer can stuff envelopes or pass out literature, but not every volunteer can design a brochure, convince corporations to make large donations, or host a fund-raising event.

SOCIAL NETWORKS FOR VOLUNTEERS

There are social networking sites that help potential volunteers determine the best fit for their age, physical abilities, locations, interests, skills, and schedules. These sites offer a variety of online tools to search organizations, access volunteer opportunities, post experiences, seek and offer advice, upload your résumé, read online newsletters, publicize upcoming events that need volunteers, find volunteer "buddies," and more.

To learn more about volunteer organizations in your area, type: *(your interest)* + *(your city)* + *volunteer* + *social networks* into your favorite search engine.

TOPICS THAT MOST NETWORKERS LIKE TO TALK ABOUT IN VOLUNTEER GROUPS

- Success stories and recognition awards
- Fund-raising events and conferences
- Celebrities who support the organization
- Pets, adoptions, and animal shelters
- Children and grandchildren
- Community services
- Youth groups and sports teams
- Volunteer jobs and recruiting
- Museums, hospitals, and rehab centers

- Education and children's services
- Government funding and medical research
- Books and movies about the organization
- Day care, neighborhoods, and schools
- Fraternal organizations and civic clubs

CONVERSATION TIP FOR ALL NETWORKING STYLES

Listen on a Deeper Level

Mentoring is one of the most rewarding ways to volunteer and follows the rise in popularity of personal coaches in today's workplace. One critical key to a successful mentor-mentee relationship is the ability to listen, not just for facts, details, and meanings, but for personal development and connections on a deeper lever. Here are things to listen for to build your bonds with others:

- Listen for mutual motivations behind actions and goals.
- Listen for the words that indicate joy and enthusiasm.
- Listen for examples of trust and mutual respect.
- Listen for the fears that create roadblocks and procrastination.
- Listen for false assumptions that lead to misunderstandings.
- Listen for good ideas and acknowledge them.
- Listen for examples of behavior that indicate progress toward overall development.
- Listen for positive reinforcement and acknowledgment of a job well done.
- Listen for commitment and gratitude.

OPENING LINES IN VOLUNTEER GROUPS

"What made you decide to volunteer for this organization?"

"Where do you think might be a good place to begin my experience as a volunteer?"

"What skills do you have to offer that are most beneficial to this organization?"

"What kind of volunteer work are you interested in?"

"What volunteering have you found most rewarding?"

"I read a really interesting story about a volunteer who . . . ."

"I volunteer for this organization because it makes me feel better about myself. I know that I am helping to make a difference in my community."

CONVERSATIONAL BRIDGES TO BUSINESS TOPICS

"What I do for this organization I also do professionally."

"Before I started my own company, I worked with small nonprofit organizations like this."

🚫 TABOO TOPICS AT VOLUNTEER ORGANIZATIONS 🚫

✗ politics (unless it is a political organization)

✗ religion (unless there is a religious affiliation)

✗ bad press or scandal about the organization or its leaders ✗ negative comments about a competitive organization ✗ overzealous proselytizing to nonmembers ✗ organization failures ✗ critical comments about a volunteer's performance ✗ overt marketing or self-promotion

---

"Do you know if this organization hires outside consultants?"
"Once I retire from . . . , I'm going to volunteer helping
people who want to change careers."

NETWORKING AND VOLUNTEERING ARE BOTH ABOUT BUILDING GOODWILL

You learned in this chapter that small talk in volunteer situations
can help you learn about people's values, goals, principles, ideas,
feelings, and opinions. You now know that once you have identified areas of commonality, you can expand the conversation
into areas where your business interests and goodwill may overlap, and then explore possible opportunities that may result in
big deals.

28

Fund-Raising Events

Donating your time for a good cause at a special event and meeting new people? What a great way to help others and network with people with whom you share philanthropic values. Networking at a fund-raising event provides you with an opportunity to establish commonality and build rapport with others you may not otherwise have the opportunity to meet. Plus, it shows that you are person who gives—and what better message to send to a prospective client?

Since fund-raising events can range from golf tournaments to black-tie dinners, be prepared to chat about business and general interest topics, but not necessarily in that order. Asking people why they support the organization can lead to a personal and revealing conversation because people often donate to the charities that help and support their families or friends. Building rapport based on personal issues can lead to even stronger business connections.

SOCIAL NETWORKING FOR FUND-RAISERS

Fund-raisers, whether their efforts are on behalf of nonprofits, nongovernment organizations, social causes, or political candidates, thrive on networking relationships. The more like-minded people fund-raisers can bring together and network, the more money they will raise, and that is where social networking holds a tremendous potential. There are social networking sites that utilize blogs, podcasts, and other constantly evolving online tools to make it easier for members to collaborate, publicize events, solicit contributions, share information, search for potential supporters, mobilize support, find volunteers, influence policy, promote legislation, lobby political representatives, build relationships with related organizations, and more.

To find out more about fund-raising, type: *social networking + fund-raising* into your favorite search engine.

TOPICS THAT MOST NETWORKERS LIKE TO TALK ABOUT AT FUND-RAISING EVENTS

- Other fund-raising events
- Keynote speakers
- Celebrity donors
- Organization's mission, accomplishments, and leadership
- Charity tax issues
- Scientific and medical advancements
- Organization's upcoming events
- Organization's success stories
- Professional fund-raising techniques
- Philanthropic organizations
- Fund-raising ideas and grant writing

- Fund-raising guidelines and ethics
- Government involvement and support

CONVERSATION TIP FOR ALL NETWORKING STYLES

Keep Your Conversations Focused on the Positive

If you are like most people at fund-raising events, you are passionate about the causes you support. However, some people may be tempted to slip into a gloomy conversation. Take care to keep your conversations focused on how people have benefited from particular activities and people.

OPENING LINES AT FUND-RAISING EVENTS

To Charity Volunteers

"What are some of the services this charity provides?"

"What do you think accounts for the increase in donations this year?"

"I'm sure you must know many great stories about people who have benefited from this organization."

To Charity Officials or Fund-Raisers

"Fund-raising must be very rewarding. How did you get started?"

"How does one set up a charitable organization?"

"I looked at your organization's Web site—it's impressive!"

Conversational Bridges to Business Topics

"I know someone who may be interested in sponsoring an event for your organization."

"What's the best way for people to find out more about how they can contribute?"

"Do you ever hire professional fund-raisers? If so, I know someone who can help you."

"Who else from the corporate world supports the work of this organization?"

🚫 Taboo Topics at Fund-Raising Events 🚫

✗ unethical fund-raising schemes ✗ misappropriation of charity funds ✗ charity event horror stories ✗ political infighting ✗ negative press about the organization ✗ criticizing competing organizations ✗ criticizing charity management ✗ discussing confidential board business ✗ pestering for a donation ✗ pushing "guilt buttons" ✗ telling people their donations to other organizations are a waste of money

---

FUND-RAISING AND NETWORKING FOCUS ON ACHIEVING BIG GOALS

You have learned in this chapter that people who attend fund-raising events like to think big, network about goal-oriented projects, and talk about what they have accomplished or hope to achieve. You now know to share your dreams as well so others understand what motivates you and where your business interests and goals coincide. It is in this area of commonality that you can work together to make big deals happen.

29

Golf Courses

According to many business experts, playing golf is an indispensable networking tool that gives people an opportunity to get to know one another in an informal environment. "After all," says Steve Cook, owner of Golf Ent, an online golf store based in Seal Beach, California, "where else can you, after four or five hours of playing together, become good friends or clients? It sure beats sitting down at a sales meeting in a sterile office!" Networking is such a natural by-product of golf that many companies look for club memberships on employees' résumés so they can entertain clients and prospect for new business on the golf course.

Business golf experts swear that the game also offers an insight into a person's way of doing business. They say a person's golf game clearly reveals how he or she solves problems, makes decisions, recovers from setbacks, deals with successes, operates under pressure, and handles competition—in short his or her character and ethics. Yet, perhaps most important is how well you take advantage of the opportunities to connect with the other players. It is during the frequent long periods between shots where much of the chatting, networking, and business take place on the golf course.

Golf etiquette includes not just how you conduct yourself as far as the playing of the game is concerned, but also how you network and conduct business while you are on the links. According to experts, if you bring up business on the first hole, relentlessly pump people for inside information, or pressure them for contacts or a sale, they probably will not be eager to play with you again—which translates to "no business." The primary purpose of playing golf with potential customers or clients is to have fun, build rapport, and get to know one another so that when you do conduct business you both feel more comfortable entering into a deal.

SOCIAL NETWORKING FOR GOLFERS

With the ever-increasing popularity of golf, the number of social networking sites devoted to the sport continues to provide a great opportunity for networkers who want to reach this generally affluent audience of players and equipment and service providers. In addition to building new business relationships and interacting more efficiently online with other golfers and vendors, these sites offer members an opportunity to post comments and pictures, read equipment and course reviews, find local tournaments and instructors, get playing tips, tee times, and find courses for business travelers. There even are dating services for single golfers.

To learn more about golf tournaments and available players in your area, type: *(your city)* + *social networking* + *golf* into your favorite search engine.

TOPICS THAT MOST NETWORKERS LIKE TO TALK ABOUT ON THE GOLF COURSE

- Business opportunities and investments
- Golf handicaps, techniques, and lessons
- Golf courses, equipment, and gadgets
- Professional and amateur golfers
- Pro and college sports
- Fashion and culture
- Home decoration and renovation
- Computers and entertainment systems
- Hobbies, pets, and gardening
- Food, wine, and spirits
- Kids, college, and schools
- Cooking and dining out
- Travel, leisure, health, and fitness
- Luxury cars, boats, and airplanes

Here are a few more conversation tips, based on networking style, for when you play golf:

Competitive Networkers. Be informal, but, depending on your partners, moderate or eliminate your expletives.

Outgoing Networkers. Talk less and play faster.

Amiable Networkers. Make enough light conversation to give your partners an opportunity to get to know you.

Analytical Networkers. Keep your games friendly—don't take winning the game so seriously that your partners won't want to play (or conduct business) with you again.

OPENING LINES ON THE GOLF COURSE

"What do you think of this course?"

"How did you decide which clubs to buy?"

"Other than golf, what hobbies do you have?"

"Do you play golf when you travel on business?"

"What insights or surprises have you learned about the businesspeople you have played with?"

"What made you decide to take up golf?"

"Can you recommend a good place to take lessons?"

"What do you do to improve your game?"

"How do you go about preventing golf injuries?"

CONVERSATIONAL BRIDGES TO BUSINESS TOPICS

"While we're waiting, do you want to hear a thumbnail sketch of our plans for next year?"

"Do you mind if I ask you a business-related question?"

"I have another client who I'd like you to meet. How about we play a round together?"

"Would you mind very much if I asked you a technical question in your area of expertise?"

⃠ TABOO TOPICS ON GOLF COURSES ⃠

✘ arguing politics ✘ clubhouse gossip ✘ competition bashing ✘ anxiety-provoking subjects ✘ quibbling over "mulligans," "gimmies" and other golf rules or etiquette ✘ unsolicited coaching ✘ personal or financial problems ✘ complaining about or blaming course conditions, equipment, caddies or others for poor games ✘ golfers who don't know or care about the rules of etiquette

GOLF AND SMALL TALK CAN YIELD BIG DEALS

In this chapter you learned some of the small talk that golfers enjoy, how to tactfully bring up business issues without taking the fun out of the game, and some golf etiquette no-nos. You now know that successful networking on the golf course is more about building business relationships than booming drives, sinking putts, or winning. When you help your partners get low scores and have a great outing, then you are well on your way to making a networking hole in one!

30

Hobby Clubs

Book clubs, model railroad clubs, chess clubs, Scrabble clubs, quilting and sewing clubs—you name an interest or pastime and there's a club for it filled with enthusiastic people who very likely spend considerable time, and possibly money, pursuing their passion. And, if you join their club, what better place to make small talk, network, and, depending on your business or career goals, maybe find a big deal.

The great thing about hobby clubs is that you don't need to live in the same city, or even the same country, to make contact and network with others who share your passionate pastimes. Thanks to the Internet, you can get the latest information on hobby club Web sites, meet people in hobby club chat rooms, and build friendships with people all over the world through e-mail. When you attend hobby club events, you can meet your "e-pen-pals" face to face, make new friends, and, of course, network even more.

SOCIAL NETWORKING FOR HOBBYISTS AND GAMERS

Whether you grow or sell orchids, build or repair model trains, or compete in online video or word game competitions, searching keywords related to your favorite hobby will bring up dozens of social networking sites dedicated to your interest. In addition to meeting and building online relationships with like-minded hobbyists and vendors, these sites offer members an opportunity to share their passions, experiences, photos, suppliers, publicize local and national events and competitions, offer and review new products and services, technological developments, discuss relevant issues, articles and publications, advertise available business ventures, job openings, and list-related social networking sites.

To find hobby clubs near you, type: *(your city)* + *social networking* + *hobby* or *game* into your favorite search engine.

HOBBY-RELATED TOPICS THAT MOST NETWORKERS LIKE TO TALK ABOUT

- How they got started
- Latest projects
- Latest trends
- Making money from a hobby
- Choosing a hobby
- History of the hobby
- Costs of hobby materials
- Benefits of a hobby
- Finding other hobbyists
- Events, workshops, and awards

Hobbyists love to play the expert, share information, and offer assistance. Here are ways to ask for or offer advice to hobbyists based on the four networking styles:

Competitive Networkers rarely admit that they need help, but will comply with requests for assistance from others if they are sure their involvement will not take too long or be too complicated. To ask a Competitive Networker for assistance say, "Can you help me . . . ? I promise it won't take but a minute."

Outgoing Networkers are not shy about making requests for help and almost always willing to provide assistance as long as it can be done quickly. To offer assistance say, "If you need help, you just let me know."

Amiable Networkers can be shy about requesting help, but are usually willing to go out of their way to give assistance, if asked in a polite way. Amiable Networkers can ask for assistance by saying, "I'm sorry to trouble you, but would you mind helping me to . . . ?"

Analytical Networkers are reluctant to request help because they want to be the one to solve the problem. However, they are usually happy to give assistance if you express that you want the job done right. To offer an Analytical Networker assistance say, "If you need any additional information, just let me know."

OPENING LINES WHEN TALKING TO HOBBYISTS

"What project are you working on now?"

"Someone once said a hobby is the key to what one will do with one's future. Have you found that to be true for you?"

"I want to introduce you to someone who shares your interest in . . . ."

"What got you interested in this hobby?"

"What's involved in getting into this hobby?"

"What fascinates you so much about . . . ?"

CONVERSATIONAL BRIDGES TO BUSINESS TOPICS

"Are you looking for a business partner?"

"What are the biggest challenges in turning your hobby into a nice business?"

"I know an adult program director who is looking for someone to teach people how to get started with this hobby. Are you interested?"

⊘ Taboo Topics at Hobby Clubs ⊘

✘ badmouthing other hobbyists or their projects ✘ turning a fun conversation about your hobby into an argument ✘ being overcompetitive at a noncompetitive hobby event ✘ monopolizing discussions at a hobbyist meeting ✘ sounding like a know-it-all (even if you are an expert) ✘ talking only about how you can make money from a hobby

---

NETWORKING ABOUT YOUR HOBBIES CAN PRODUCE PROFITS

In this chapter you learned topics that hobbyists like to talk about and how to approach them based on their networking styles. You now know that if you join a hobby club and network with others who share your passion you will be on your way to turning small talk into big profits.

31

Houses of Worship

Many people prefer to socialize and do business with others who share their religious beliefs, so what better place to network than the place where they worship? Knowing that they share some beliefs makes many people feel more comfortable breaking the ice and conversing about a variety of topics, some of which may include business. However, always respect a person's desire not to discuss business on a day of worship.

Make small talk before the service, first discussing issues relating to news about friends and family, personal goals, hobbies, and other informal topics before bringing up business topics. Make sure you avoid controversial, political, or unpleasant topics. Instead, bring up topics such as the sermon, the church, synagogue, mosque, or the person conducting the service. Keep all your conversations focused on the positive and let your discourse serve as a vehicle to exchange information about one another—your hopes, dreams, goals, and endeavors. Listen carefully for keywords and implied statements that suggest a topic of interest related to your business. If the other person is interested in discussing business, don't dwell on the subject for too long. It's better to acknowledge that you have a shared interest and then agree to speak about it later, perhaps even in your or their place of business.

SOCIAL NETWORKING FOR RELIGIOUS INDIVIDUALS

Religious social networking sites bring together devotees, spiritual leaders, and faith-based communities for religious study, inspiration, music, entertainment, and interaction. They offer members opportunities to connect online with others through blogs, clubs, discussion forums, feeds, and live events. For singles who want to meet others with the same faith, some sites provide dating, introductions, counseling, and guidance services. Some religious social networking sites encourage people of all faiths to interact, while others are strictly oriented to a particular faith. Networking can be productive on faith-based social networking sites because many people prefer to do business with those who share their religion.

To find faith-based organizations, type: *(your faith)* + *social networks* into your favorite search engine.

TOPICS THAT MOST NETWORKERS LIKE TO TALK ABOUT IN HOUSES OF WORSHIP

- Specific religious doctrines
- Specific scriptures and stories
- Changes in the church
- Religious studies and history

- Religious life and ministries
- Art, architecture, and religion
- Religious rituals and holidays
- Travel to the Holy Land
- Fund-raising events and volunteerism
- Personal beliefs

CONVERSATION TIP FOR ALL NETWORKING STYLES

Discussing Religion Is Always a Touchy Subject

If you want to bring up your religion at a networking event, discuss how your faith influences your activities, goals, and values. Never preach, proselytize, or call into question the beliefs or religions of others.

OPENING LINES IN HOUSES OF WORSHIP

"What made you decide to join this (church, temple, mosque)?"

"What message did you get out of today's sermon?"

"What role do you think the (church, temple, mosque) should play in our community?"

"Have you attended other religious services?"

"In what ways has faith changed your life?"

"My neighbor also belongs to this (church, temple, mosque)."

"I've been a member of this (church, temple, mosque) for years."

"How has the membership of this (church, temple, mosque) changed over the years?"

CONVERSATIONAL BRIDGES TO BUSINESS TOPICS

"I volunteer my business services to our (church, temple, mosque)."

"I work in the travel business and know some great places to visit in the Holy Land."

"One of my colleagues also belongs to this (church, temple, mosque)."

"I'm in the advertising and printing business if you want to discuss any ideas for this year's fund-raising event."

⊘ TABOO TOPICS AT HOUSES OF WORSHIP ⊘

✕ controversial politics ✕ abortion ✕ stem cell research ✕ birth control ✕ sex and church scandals ✕ confrontational political news shows ✕ sectarian violence in the Middle East ✕ conflicts between church and government ✕ religion in public schools ✕ the Crusades and other religious wars ✕ religious cults ✕ church, temple, or mosque politics ✕ sexual preferences

---

NETWORK FOR KINDRED SPIRITS IN YOUR HOUSE OF WORSHIP

In this chapter you learned the topics that many people are willing to discuss before or after attending religious get-togethers. You now know that by networking in these situations, you will find people who not only share your religion, but who may also share similar attitudes in business, thus increasing your chances of creating big deals.

32

Reunions

If the thought of going to your high school or college reunion sends you running for cover, then consider this: Everyone changes over the years, so why worry if you've put on a little weight or lost some hair? The fact is that high school and college reunions are fun-filled social events that also offer many opportunities to *gently* network for business with people who share some of your history and who are eager to hear your updated autobiography.

After years of not seeing old classmates, it's easy to reintroduce yourself, find out what they do (or did) for a living, what they like to do now for fun, and where they spend their time, efforts, and money. Tell others the "short highlights" version of what you've been doing for the last umpteen years with only a passing reference to any bad patches. As you listen and exchange information about your current activities, goals, children, hobbies, and other pursuits, be sure to let these people know that you're still in business and that you can help them achieve their goals.

As you reconnect with old friends and classmates, take mental notes of the people and their adult kids who went into businesses similar to your customers and clients. While these folks may be your target prospects during regular business hours, at the reunion they are old classmates first and potential customers second. However, once the event is over, you can seek them out like you would any other potential customers.

SOCIAL NETWORKING FOR PEOPLE PLANNING OR ATTENDING REUNIONS

With people moving more frequently and further afield than ever before, the growth of reunion-oriented social networking sites is on the rise. These sites offer members and vendors information, services, products, resources, and links that promote and facilitate school, organization, company, and family gatherings. Some social networking sites offer free basic services that include reunion announcement, planning tips, and member searches. Other sites charge fees for more personalized services such as reunion planning, finding extended family members, long-lost friends and coworkers, travel and hotel accommodations, invitations, registration and tracking, photography, and printing of materials.

To find out more about planning or attending reunions, type: *reunion social networks* into your favorite search engine.

TOPICS THAT MOST NETWORKERS LIKE TO TALK ABOUT AT REUNIONS

- Kids and family
- Business

- Retirement
- Old and new projects
- Hobbies
- Travel
- Personal passions
- Old friends
- Alumni organizations
- Living one's dream

CONVERSATION TIPS FOR ALL NETWORKING STYLES

Seven Ways to Reconnect at Reunions

1. Be ready to give a brief answer to "What have you been doing all these years?"
2. Ask the person to join you for a cocktail, coffee, or snack, so you can have more time to talk.
3. Reconnect over old interests and forge new connections with new interests.
4. Reveal your new dreams and goals so your old friends still know what's important to you.
5. Invite old and new friends to get-togethers outside the reunion's official events.
6. Exchange more personal (but not too much!) information.
7. Say how you are going to remain in contact, and then follow through on your promise.

Here are a few more conversation tips based on networking styles when you talk to people at reunions:

Competitive Networkers. Don't brag about your accomplishments.

Outgoing Networkers. Don't tell your life story.

Amiable Networkers. Don't downplay your business dreams.

Analytical Networkers. Don't go into excruciating detail about your business.

Opening Lines at Reunions

"So tell me, what have you been doing all these years?"

"Hi! I'm . . . . We were in the same class."

"Do you know how I can get in touch with . . . ?"

"I see that you live in . . . . What's it like there?"

"This is my first reunion and is it ever interesting!"

"I can't begin to imagine how much work it must be to organize a reunion!"

"I found a genealogy Web site that helps people find their long-lost relatives."

"Do you know much about your family genealogy?"

"I'm thinking of organizing a family reunion. Do you know an organization that can help?"

CONVERSATIONAL BRIDGES TO BUSINESS TOPICS

"I read your bio in the reunion book and saw that you are in the . . . business. I'm looking for someone who does what you do."

"I'm a journalist. Have you heard any good reunion stories?"

"Do you know a hotel that can give us a good rate for our upcoming reunion?"

"My oldest daughter is in your field. Do you mind if I give her your number?"

"Since we are in the same business, do you want to get together and compare notes?"

"It never occurred to me how big the reunion business is."
"I want to create a family cookbook from our reunion.
Do you know anyone in the publishing business?"

⊘ Taboo Topics at Reunions ⊘

✗ rekindle old arguments ✗ remind others of past
indiscretions ✗ gossip about old rivals ✗ make remarks
about cosmetic surgery, age, weight, hair (or lack thereof)
✗ ask more than one question about a messy divorce
✗ talk too much about oneself ✗ flirt with an old flame
who is happily married ✗ bring up marital problems
✗ tell sad personal stories ✗ criticize the food
or reunion organizers

REUNIONS ARE OPPORTUNITIES TO NETWORK AND RECONNECT

In this chapter you learned that networking at reunions is easier
and more rewarding if you have some business-related topics
ready to introduce into your conversations. You now know that
since most people attend reunions to socialize, you shouldn't
push your networking agenda too hard until you know for sure
that the other person shares a strong desire to discuss a mutual
business interest.

33

Wedding Receptions

Wedding receptions are good places to network, but you must do so with restraint since the focus of most people there is not on business, but on having fun and celebrating the happy occasion. Be sure to introduce yourself to everyone seated at your table. It's easier to break the ice by walking around the table, introducing yourself, and chatting for a minute or so before you take your seat for the meal. Once you sit down and before you get into any longer discourse with your companion, continue to engage new acquaintances seated close to you.

If you're just meeting for the first time, focus most of your conversations on topics related to the bride, groom, and their families. When someone asks, "What do you do?" offer a brief description how you help people and then ask in return, "What about you?" This way you can bring up the topics of business without sounding like you are trolling for customers or clients. If people do not ask about your profession or business, then wait until a subject comes up where you can easily drop in a word or two about what you do and then, if someone shows an interest in hearing more, bridge to a business topic.

SOCIAL NETWORKS FOR THE WEDDING PLANNERS

Wedding-focused social networking sites allow couples, wedding planners, and vendors to compare the plethora of nuptial-related services, including bridal gown and tuxedo rentals, do-it-yourself wedding invitations, online registries, venues, catering, and more. Most of these social networking sites also allow members to post comments about vendors and products, introduce their wedding parties, share stories, offer forums and advice for prenuptial agreements and other related issues, provide images, sample speeches, and toasts, and even help create a customized Web site. Forums and blogs on these sites offer great networking opportunities for anyone who services the wedding industry.

To find out more about planning weddings, type: *wedding planners* + *social networks* into your favorite search engine.

TOPICS THAT MOST NETWORKERS LIKE TO TALK ABOUT AT WEDDING RECEPTIONS

- Personal or funny stories about relatives
- Updates on family members
- Genealogy and family histories
- Stories about ancestors
- Media stories and books about families
- Food, catering, and home entertainment
- Weddings, honeymoons, and travel
- Children and child-rearing practices
- Love, marriage, and relationships

- Family reunions and finding relatives
- Businesses, entrepreneurs, and careers
- Money and lifestyle
- Celebrity marriages
- Home-improvement
- Real estate and retirement

CONVERSATION TIP FOR ALL NETWORKING STYLES

Ten Things Never to Say at a Wedding Reception

Before you go to the wedding reception, take a minute and consider topics you are willing to discuss with the other guests. Keep them light, fun, and upbeat! Since you never know to whom you might be talking, *never say*:

1. "I hope this marriage lasts longer than his/her last one."
2. "If you ask me, they're making a big mistake."
3. "This will be the happiest day of their lives. It's all downhill from here."
4. "His/her ex was a lot better looking and had more money, too!"
5. "This food isn't as good as the food at the last wedding I went to."
6. "I hate cheap champagne. Oh well, beggars can't be choosers!"
7. "I bet this wedding and reception cost a bundle. How can they afford it?"
8. "I wonder if she is . . . well, you know . . . ."
9. "She's wearing white? I don't think so!"
10. "No doubt about it—she/he married him/her for the money."

OPENING LINES AT WEDDING RECEPTIONS

"We haven't seen each other in twenty years, but I'd recognize you anywhere."

"I really want to get to know my new family's friends. Tell me, when did you first meet?"

"I don't believe we've met, but any friend of . . . is a friend of mine."

"I'm so delighted to see you. What do you think of the happy couple?"

"I'm really impressed with everything, especially the food!"

"This reception is different from all the other wedding receptions I've attended."

"Are you friends of the bride or groom?"

CONVERSATIONAL BRIDGES TO BUSINESS TOPICS

"It's always been my dream to do what you do. I'd love to know how you got started."

"The groom's mother mentioned that you are looking for . . . . I may be able to help you."

"I made the travel arrangements for the couple's honeymoon. It's one of my specialties."

"The father of the bride is one of my clients."

⊘ TABOO TOPICS AT WEDDING RECEPTIONS ⊘

✗ divorce ✗ messy personal relationships
✗ complaining about unhappy marriages ✗ pregnancy, fertility, abortion, and unhappy stories about children
✗ past relationships of the bride or groom ✗ old flames of the bride or groom ✗ family secrets ✗ in-law troubles

USE NETWORKING OPPORTUNITIES AT WEDDING RECEPTIONS TO BUILD RELATIONSHIPS

You've learned in this chapter that some topics are safe to bring up at wedding receptions while there are others that you most certainly want to avoid! Now that you know when to converse with guests from both sides of the family and how to transition to business subjects, you'll have more opportunities to turn small talk into big deals.

PART V

PUBLIC SITUATIONS: OPENING LINES, TOPICS, AND NETWORKING STRATEGIES

34

Four Rules of Networking Etiquette in Public Situations

I can't think of a better word to describe why I like to network in public situations than "serendipity"—which according to the Wikipedia definition is "the effect by which one accidentally discovers something fortunate, especially while looking for or doing something else entirely." Networking in public provides opportunities to connect with people whom you may not ordinarily mix with in your typical business, social, or personal circles. Once you make small talk and connect with people through chance encounters in public situations, you can't help but increase your contacts who may lead to big deals. Here are a few points about each networking style, including topics to bring up and subjects and phrases to avoid while networking in public situations:

Competitive Networkers are usually open to contact in public situations because they know that the stranger seated next to them on the airplane may be a potential client or customer. However, because they frequently read or work in public situations, interrupting them with a phrase such as "Nice weather we're having, don't you think?" will likely earn you only a curt, "I suppose so." "Are you traveling for business or pleasure?" will probably get a more favorable response.

Outgoing Networkers take pride in being able to talk to just about anyone in any public situation. They are open to most topics on business, culture, or family, so you can use practically any opening line except ones that focus on gory crimes or disasters. However, if you'd rather read or work than talk, still offer a friendly greeting. After a few comments or questions, open your book or your laptop and excuse yourself from the conversation.

Amiable Networkers may be reluctant to make contact with others in public situations unless the people are at least somewhat familiar. Bringing up general and non-threatening topics will allay some of their fear of talking to strangers, but they will still be cautious. Never launch into a sales pitch, complain about travel, or bring up unpleasant topics.

Analytical Networkers may hesitate to make contact with others in public situations unless they feel that the people share their interests. They are usually willing to respond to questions or comments that are technical in nature although a phrase such as "Don't you think . . . ?" will probably come across as confrontational. Also, avoid topics that are personal or controversial.

1. Respect a Person's Right to Privacy

Although "public" means sharing space with other people in the community, some people just don't want to talk to you—or anyone else for that matter, particularly about business. Repeated attempts to engage people who are not interested in conversation are generally considered rude and unwelcome. Competitive and Outgoing Networkers need to pay particular attention to this rule because others may feel threatened by what they see as aggressive overtures.

2. Never Discuss Personal Topics with Strangers

Striking up an informal conversation with a stranger seated next to you in an airport, at a sporting event, doctor's office, or other public place is generally considered an acceptable and friendly form of contact as long as the topics, questions, or self-disclosures are not of a personal nature. Outgoing Networkers need to pay particular attention to this rule because others may feel that it is inappropriate to be overly familiar with strangers.

3. Respect a Stranger's "Personal Space"

How close should you stand when you engage a stranger in conversation? The answer often depends on the person's ethnic background and his or her overall comfort level talking to strangers. In general, while there are many exceptions, most cultures prefer conversations at about arm's length, with Asians a bit more than arm's length and Hispanic and Middle Easterners a bit less. All networkers need to pay particular attention to this rule.

4. Networking Is Connecting—Not Selling

While most success-oriented people often exchange business information with people they meet in public, most view an overt sales pitch from a stranger as unprofessional and unwelcome. Therefore, look to make a connection, not a sale, when networking in public. Competitive and Outgoing Networkers need to pay particular attention to this rule so they don't come across as too aggressive to strangers.

FOLLOWING NETWORKING ETIQUETTE IN PUBLIC SITUATIONS CREATES FEELINGS OF SERENDIPITY

In this chapter you learned that the trick to networking in public situations is to be friendly yet respectful by not violating another person's privacy or personal space, revealing any personal problems, or shamelessly pitching your products or service. When you follow these guidelines and others say, "What a fortunate coincidence that we met!" then you can easily segue to business-related conversations. Now you are ready to learn how to apply these principles to networking in common public situations.

35

Neighborhoods

"**H**ello, Neighbor!" When you talk to the people you see on a regular basis in your neighborhood, making new friends and great networking contacts is easy. If you haven't already, introduce yourself to an acquaintance or newcomer to your neighborhood. The relationship starts simply enough—a friendly hello and, after a little while, an introduction and an informal conversation. You will be surprised that, in a relatively short time, you can go from being a nameless stranger down the block to a friend and neighbor, and with that new status comes many benefits. Neighbors typically give and receive referrals to the people who live nearby because they know, like, and trust them.

As in any successful networking relationship, it's what you offer neighbors that establishes rapport and creates an incentive for others to reciprocate in some way. Since neighbors share many needs and interests, don't hesitate to offer help or assistance when you can. Whether it's giving your neighbor the name and telephone number of your plumber, suggesting a great place to buy plants, or helping unload a pickup truck full of building supplies, you can easily position yourself as a resource to your neighbors—without going overboard or becoming overly involved.

In return, there may come a time when you will call upon them for their advice, assistance, or, perhaps, even their business. Yes, there are some neighbors who may not be receptive to you or just prefer to stick to themselves, and that is something that you need to respect. However, with time and a light conversational touch, even shy neighbors can warm up and become good networking contacts.

CONNECTING WITH PEOPLE IN YOUR NEIGHBORHOOD VIA SOCIAL NETWORKS

Neighborhood-oriented social networking services are proliferating at a remarkable rate and with a variety of features. These services allow you to locate and communicate with your circle of existing and potential friends within a given geographical location using text and instant messaging on a cell phone or laptop. Some social networking sites built specifically for mobile phones where you can "ping" your friends or associates with your whereabouts, lets you know when your friends are nearby, allows you to broadcast content to anyone within a few blocks of you, or blast messages to your groups of friends. Others connect members of a group or community, from any Internet-enabled handset, so they never miss a chance to network in person. They provide a directory that works like radar to give any group of people the ability to detect, search, browse, and connect to one another when they happen to be in the same city and as close as a few blocks away.

> To find out what's going on in your neighborhood, type: *(your neighborhood + city) + social networks* into your favorite search engine.

Here are a few conversation tips based on networking styles for making small talk with your neighbors:

Competitive Networkers. Rather than challenging your neighbor with a competitive comment such as "I think my . . . is better than yours because . . . ," say, "When I saw your beautiful new . . . it really inspired me to . . . ."

Outgoing Networkers. Don't let short chats about banal topics turn into longwinded stories about banal topics.

Amiable Networkers. To send friendly signals and show your willingness to chat with a neighbor, ask him or her an easy-to-answer question about a pet, recent renovation, or neighborhood-related issue.

Analytical Networkers. When a neighbor proudly shows you his or her recent home improvement or newly purchased appliance, unless you are asked for your professional opinion, keep any critical comments to yourself. Just say, "That looks great!"

TOPICS THAT NEIGHBORS WHO ARE NETWORKERS LIKE TO TALK ABOUT

- Gardens and home improvement
- Renovation contractors
- Real estate prices and rental market
- Local stores, food shops, and restaurants

- Hardware supplies and tools
- Cars, motorcycles, and boats
- Food and home entertainment
- Old and new neighbors
- Schools, kids, family, and pets
- Local recreation and parks
- Pro, college, and amateur sports
- Appliances, entertainment systems, and computers

Opening Lines in Your Neighborhood

"Where did you live before you moved here?"

"So, what do you think of the neighborhood?"

"Can you recommend a good electrician?"

"I really admire your beautiful garden! What do you do to get those flowers to grow so tall?"

"What kind of dog is that? She's a beauty!"

"I heard the house down the street sold for . . . ."

"I just met the new people who moved in across the street. They seem friendly."

Conversational Bridges to Business Topics

"I see you head off to work every morning. What kind of work do you do?"

"I've been working from home for years. I'm in the . . . business."

"I can see from all the work you've done on your house you really know what you're doing. Where did you learn all those skills? Do you work in the trades?"

"If you ever need somebody for . . . , I've been in the business for years."

🚫 Taboo Topics in Your Neighborhood 🚫

✗ referring friends instead of competent tradespeople
✗ badmouthing or spreading rumors about other
neighbors ✗ complaining about minor annoyances
✗ offering unsolicited advice ✗ criticizing a neighbor's
decorating ✗ criticizing a neighbor's choice
of contractors ✗ asking overly personal questions
✗ pressuring neighbors to buy products or services
you sell ✗ race- or religion-based slurs or jokes

GOOD NEIGHBORS MAKE FOR GOOD NETWORKING!

In this chapter you learned that by making small talk and steadily building your personal relationships with your neighbors—while respecting their privacy and guarding your own—you'll find out if and where your business interests overlap. You now know that if you have built that trusted relationship, your neighbors may be open to discuss business issues or offer referrals to others who can help you achieve big deals.

36

Airplanes and Trains

If you are among the record number of "road warriors" traveling for work by air or train these days, you have a great opportunity to network for business while you travel. You can network with people in check-in lines, waiting areas, snack bars, gift shops, restaurants, and, of course, with the people seated next to you or where other passengers congregate. As you enter the waiting area, look for other business travelers working on their laptops, reading reports, or talking on their cell phones before departure. They may be good prospects.

When you are seated, offer a friendly smile and polite hello to the person or people next to you. If they are not occupied, take a risk and break the ice with a ritual question like, "Are you traveling today for business or pleasure?" or "Are you traveling back home today or away?" Your objective is to let the other person know that you are friendly and willing to talk and, if he or she is interested, engage in a light conversation.

If he or she returns your overture with a friendly response, then you've broken the ice and your conversation is off and running. However, if after you say hello, you receive a curt nod and the person returns to his or her work, reading, or nap, don't be offended. Simply, take out some work or reading material of your own so it is obvious that you, too, are traveling for business. If you can do it without being too obvious, glance at the person's papers or overhear his or her phone calls to learn more about his or her profession or area of business. When the time is right—that is, when he or she glances up, says something to you, or when the flight or train attendant offers a snack—you can again attempt to start a conversation based on what you see the person working on or reading, an earlier conversation, or your destination.

SOCIAL NETWORKING FOR TRAVELERS

Travel social networking sites allow travelers to build their own communities and offer each other travel advice, packing suggestions, feedback about destinations, methods of transportation, sites to see, local etiquette, and customs, links to top travel-related sites, articles, blogs, pictures, videos, polls and deals, weather alerts, traveling companions, and more. Some of these sites allow members to keep track of their travels, share their photos, reviews, and blogs with friends and family, as well as research destinations before booking a trip.

To learn more about travel-related topics or events near you, type: *travel + (place) + social network sites* into your favorite search engine.

TOPICS THAT MOST NETWORKERS LIKE TO TALK ABOUT WHILE ON AIRPLANES AND TRAINS

- Travel tips and bargains
- Best seats, perks, and security

- Interesting road-warrior stories
- Great hotels and restaurants
- Resorts and vacation spots
- Computers and technology
- Companies, economics, and business
- Business projects, goals, and contacts
- Travel, other cultures, politics, and news (with care)
- Home, family, and hobbies
- Sports, cars, and power tools
- Movies, books, TV, and pop culture
- Good-humored pet peeves of air travel

CONVERSATION TIPS FOR ALL NETWORKERS

Guessing a Stranger's Networking Style Based on His or Her Recommendation

Not only are recommendations for restaurants, computers, software, places to visit, books, and countless other things great opening lines that allow people to share with you what they like and feel strongly about, but they can help you zero in on a person's networking style. After asking for a recommendation, listen carefully not only for the answer, but also for whether the recommendation reflects status, popularity, value, or functionality.

Recommendations from Competitive Networkers tend to reflect status. For example, "If you want the best brand of . . . then buy . . . ."

Recommendations from Outgoing Networkers tend to reflect popularity. For example, "Everyone loves this . . . ."

Recommendations from Amiable Networkers tend to reflect value. For example, "The place is excellent for the price."

> **Recommendations from Analytical Networkers tend to reflect functionality.** For example, "It's not the best looking or the most popular, but you can't beat it when it comes to performance."

Opening Lines on Airplanes and on Trains

> "I'm headed to a convention in . . . . Have you been there before?"
>
> "Are you on the way home or away?"
>
> "I've never been to . . . before, but I understand it's got some great restaurants. Can you recommend a good place to eat dinner and maybe spend a few hours sightseeing in . . . ?"
>
> "I see you smiling (groaning) at the headline on the sports (business, front, etc.) page. What do you think of . . . ?"

Conversational Bridges to Business Topics

> "I travel this route a lot for business. What about you?"
>
> "I see your shirt (briefcase, etc.) has a . . . logo on it. Do you work for that company?"

⃠ TABOO TOPICS ON AIRPLANES AND TRAINS ⃠

✘ travel disasters ✘ pilot stress and substance abuse ✘ passenger air sickness stories ✘ travel hassles and lost baggage ✘ terrorism, hijacking, or 9-11 ✘ telling your life story ✘ complaints about the airline or train food and service ✘ asking for too much professional advice ✘ seeking proprietary information

---

"What kind of projects do you work on?"

"What do you see as the biggest challenges to getting your projects done on time and on budget?"

NETWORKING WHILE TRAVELING IS BASED ON RECEPTIVITY, RAPPORT, AND LUCK

In this chapter you learned that if you are the first to break the ice with other travelers, you can quickly determine if they are open to more conversation and to networking. You now know also how to guess a stranger's networking style based on his or her recommendations for a restaurant, club, or activity. Like all networking encounters in public, it's in part luck, rapport, and receptivity that allow small talk with fellow travelers to segue into conversations that can lead to big deals.

37

Bars and Restaurant Counters

If you are like many people these days, you prefer chatting with other patrons at sushi bars or restaurant counters instead of eating alone in silence at a table. Whether you stop for breakfast on your way to the office, grab a bite to eat for lunch, or have dinner at your favorite diner or tapas bar after a day of work, this relaxed style of dining creates an atmosphere that makes it easy to break the ice and talk to strangers seated near you. You can bring up topics such as restaurants, ethnic cuisine, cooking, travel, sports, and, of course, business. In most cases, it doesn't take long to build rapport and discover common general and business interests. Once you do, your opportunities to network for business are only limited by your ability to connect and communicate.

For example, at a sushi bar, start your conversation with a chef, manager, staff, or owner by letting him or her know that you appreciate the skill that goes into food preparation and that you are interested and respectful of Japanese traditions. Since others dining at the sushi bar will undoubtedly overhear your conversation (eavesdropping is part of the dining experience at sushi bars), you're also sending them the message that you are willing to talk and have an interest in Japanese cuisine and culture.

Of course, whether you're dining at a bar or a restaurant counter, never forget your manners when you first approach a nearby patron. Offer a nod, a smile, and a polite hello and see how the person responds. If he or she gives you a warm greeting in return, then consider it a green light to opening the conversation with an easy-to-answer question or comment about the food, restaurant, sports, or other light subject. However, if the person gives you a curt response and immediately buries his or her head in a book or newspaper, then be respectful of his or her privacy, and look for someone else to talk to.

SOCIAL NETWORKING SITES FOR WINE LOVERS

Many social networking sites for wine lovers offer members an opportunity to recommend and rate wines as well as wine shops and wineries; read and post reviews; compare prices; manage wine collections; create a list of wines they want to try; list wines they want to buy, sell, or trade; and even track what other people on your list buy and taste. After meeting online with other wine lovers, experts, and vendors via wine blogs on social networking sites, you can network with them in person at wine tastings, industry-related events, or at wine shops.

To find more people near you who share an interest in wines, type: *(your city)* + *wine tasting* + *social networks* into your favorite search engine.

TOPICS THAT MOST NETWORKERS LIKE TO TALK ABOUT AT BARS AND RESTAURANTS

- Favorite watering holes and restaurants
- Local sports and pro teams
- Local news and politics (with care)
- Food and beverage
- Restauranteurs and food businesses
- Local businesses and opportunities
- Professions
- Local entertainment
- Local markets
- Specialty food and liquor stores

CONVERSATION TIPS FOR ALL NETWORKING STYLES

Breaking the Ice at Restaurant Counters

Eavesdrop on nearby conversations, but don't be too obvious about it until you get a signal from the person or people next to you that you are welcome into the conversation. Once you are in the conversation, don't wait too long to introduce yourself and include a bit of free information about where you are from or what you do for a living. In addition, here are tips for each networking style to help you start conversations with another solo diner while eating at a restaurant counter or bar.

Competitive Networkers. Turn off your cell phone ringer (you can keep it on vibrate) and instead engage someone nearby in a casual conversation about something you see, hear, or can refer to in your immediate surroundings. Be sure to introduce yourself.

Outgoing Networkers. Your laughter may be contagious, but keep the volume of your voice at a low to moderate level as you make small talk with others dining at the counter.

Amiable Networkers. To show people seated nearby that you are available to chat, give them a gentle smile and nod hello. If someone gives you a friendly response, make a positive comment about the food or the establishment. Follow that up with a question about the meal or recommendation for a dish.

Analytical Networkers. As you engage in small talk with someone at the counter, be sure to balance the amount of time you talk and listen and avoid any technical jargon with those who do not share your area of expertise.

Opening Lines at Restaurant Counters or Bars

"Does that . . . taste as good as it looks?"

"This is a great appetizer with that wine."

"Excuse me, what you're eating looks really good. Would you recommend it?"

"I can see you are enjoying that glass of . . . . What exactly are you drinking?"

"What other dishes have you had here that you like?"

"I was told that this restaurant is great for private parties."

Opening Lines at a Sushi Bar

"I'd like to try an authentic Japanese dish. What would you recommend?"

"I admire sushi chefs. I love watching them cut and arrange the food on the plate."

"What dishes would you recommend to an adventurous diner?"

"Have you ever visited Japan?"

"I live in the neighborhood and this is my favorite Japanese restaurant."

"Have you ever been to a sake tasting?"

"I was reading an interesting book about the origins of sushi and Japanese ingredients."

"Do you like to cook Japanese-inspired food?"

"I first fell in love with Japanese food when I . . . ."

"What is it that you like best about Japanese food?"

Conversational Bridges to Business Topics

"One of my clients here is in the . . . business."

"I'm in town on business, but I can see why people would like to live here. Do you work in the area?"

"What industry do you work in?"

⊘ TABOO TOPICS AT BARS AND RESTAURANT COUNTERS ⊘

✗ restaurant horror stories ✗ food poisoning
✗ this morning's hangover and upset stomach
✗ loud complaints about bad service ✗ sad or
unpleasant news stories ✗ unhappy relationships
✗ medical maladies or recent surgeries ✗ World War II
(at sushi bars) ✗ unappetizing food preparation stories
✗ crime ✗ *E. coli* outbreaks ✗ famine

"If you like to buy . . . , I can recommend a great place
to shop."

"I recently took a great seminar on doing business with
Japanese companies."

"I think there are many ways Japanese and American companies can work together."

NETWORKING AT RESTAURANT COUNTERS AND BARS CAN LEAD TO PROFITABLE CONVERSATIONS

In this chapter, you learned how to break the ice and get other
diners at restaurant counters engaged in conversation. You also
now know how to introduce a variety of small-talk topics that
help you quickly build trust and rapport and uncover common
business or networking interests. Once you make the transition
from small talk to business topics, suggest exchanging business
cards and you'll be a small step closer to making a big deal.

38

Health Clubs and Spas

"**W**ow! You're looking great!" Whether you lift weights, swim, play a sport, or relax in a steam bath, health clubs and spas are great places to network because people there are usually disciplined and focused on self-improvement. They are people who tend to set and achieve goals and possibly make decisions as team leaders. Also, as with most successful business-people, they strive to make improvements and understand that it takes consistent work over a period of time to get results.

Although you may find out a person's occupation early on in your conversation, first talk about other general topics before delving too deeply into his or her business. As you talk about your mutual interests in fitness, health, and sports, be sure to drop in a few keywords about your business and how you help others. If the other person expresses interest in your business or profession, then moving the conversation to business topics will not be a problem as long as you don't turn your conversation into a sales call.

Note that many people consider their time at the health club or spa as private and prefer to workout or relax without having to chat with anyone. You can still offer a friendly hello, but don't bother trying to network. If you see someone on a regular basis, he or she may, in time, warm up to you and be willing to engage in conversation. Once that happens, there may be an opportunity, albeit a slight one, to network.

SOCIAL NETWORKING SITES FOR PEOPLE WHO JUST WANT TO PLAY

Sports-oriented social networking Web sites are online meeting places where sports participants, enthusiasts, and organizations can find each other, communicate, and meet up in person to play sports and related activities. These social networking sites help sports enthusiasts find players, workout partners, teams, games, tournaments, leagues, facilities, coaches, instructors, schools, camps, clinics, gyms, pools, and nearly everything else they might be looking for in their particular sport. Dozens of these sites list hundreds of sports and activities in regions across the United States.

To find out more sports-related activities near you, type: *(your city)* + *amateur sports* + *social networks* into your favorite search engine.

TOPICS THAT MOST NETWORKERS LIKE TO TALK ABOUT AT HEALTH CLUBS AND SPAS

- Social and professional dancing
- Marathons
- Martial arts events .

- Pro and amateur sporting events
- Health products
- Sporting goods stores
- Fitness equipment
- Diet and nutrition
- Clothes and fashion
- Cooking and restaurants

CONVERSATION TIPS FOR ALL NETWORKERS

Chat Etiquette in the Gym

- Don't interrupt people while they are exercising.
- When you do talk, speak in a quiet voice.
- Keep your conversations short.
- Respect a person's desire not to engage in conversation.

Opening Lines at Health Clubs and Spas

"I'm new here. Would you mind showing me how to adjust this machine?"

"How long have you been a member of this club?"

"What's your secret to staying so fit?"

"What do you think of the facilities and staff here?"

"Excuse me, it looks like we lift the same amount of weight. Would you mind if I alternate sets with you?"

"I can see you are waiting for this machine. This is my last set and then it's all yours."

"We always schedule our workouts at the same time. Do you want to spot each other on the weights and machines?"

Conversational Bridges to Business Topics

"I notice that you're taking advantage of our company's corporate fitness center every morning, too. I work in the . . . department. What about you?"

"I'm a fitness trainer and nutritionist. I help people change their behavior patterns and choose more healthy lifestyles."

"Do you have a professional interest in this area, too?"

"What keeps you busy when you're not working out?"

"I'm in the . . . business. What about you?"

"If you are interested in home gym equipment or a personal trainer, let me know."

⊘ Taboo Topics at Health Clubs and Spas ⊘

✘ criticizing the appearance of others ✘ medical problems ✘ personal relationships with staff or other members ✘ facilities-related ailments ✘ gossiping about members or staff ✘ sexual innuendoes ✘ patronizing comments

---

STAY FIT OR RELAX WHILE YOU NETWORK FOR BUSINESS CONTACTS

In this chapter you learned how to use small talk to open the channels of communication with others as they workout or relax at health clubs or spas. You now know that many of these people are goal-oriented and that they are probably open to exploring business issues that can lead to big deals for themselves and for you.

39

Sporting Events

"**P**lay ball!" When you sit next to people at a baseball game, tennis match, or other sporting event, striking up a conversation with them is easy. After all, it's hard to find people more passionate than sports fans. You can talk to them about the game, players, managers, and sports in general, but you can also chat about your families, interests, and business topics, too—what you do, who you know, and who you've worked with. All the while, not only are you building rapport and likability—two key elements in establishing a networking relationship—but you can assess, how you can help this person and how he or she can help you?"

Savvy networkers invite clients and potential customers to attend tournaments and sporting events so they can get to know one another better and talk business in an informal situation, but also so their clients can meet and network with other new contacts. Once you define your common interests, needs, and values with those you meet and take to sporting events, the potential to help one another through networking increases.

SOCIAL NETWORKING FOR THE
PROFESSIONAL SPORTS FAN

If you live for professional sports or work in a related business, there are numerous social networking sites that can help you keep up with this fast-paced industry. Many of these social networking sites combine sports business news, blogs, articles, resources, and trends along with forums that offer members the insights of the brightest minds from professional sports teams, leagues, sponsors, agencies, and consultants. Online discussion forums allow members to share their views about a wide variety of professional sports related issues, including how sponsors, teams, and others can take advantage of the increasing popularity of blogs, user-generated content, video, widgets, chat, and social networking to drive fan loyalty, ticket sales, and revenue.

To find out about sporting events nearby or people with whom you share an interest in a particular sport, type: *(sport) + professional sports fans + social networks* into your favorite search engine.

TOPICS THAT MOST NETWORKERS LIKE TO TALK ABOUT AT SPORTING EVENTS

- Economic impact of local sports teams
- Local pro, college, school team games
- Health and fitness
- Sports clubs and activities
- Marathons and personal workouts
- Favorite athletes and sports icons

- College sports and emerging athletes
- Sports memorabilia and card collecting
- Sports-related businesses
- Skiing, tennis, golf, and individual sports
- Sporting equipment
- Adventure vacations
- Extreme sports
- Olympic games
- Sports statistics and books
- Internet and all-sports talk shows

CONVERSATION TIPS FOR ALL NETWORKING STYLES

Don't Get Trapped by Trash Talk

And you think people get upset when they argue about politics! Discussions on that topic seem mild compared to how some avid sports fans get when they encounter their arch-rival fan at a networking event. Rather than get into a noisy and aggressive battle over teams, coaches, players, or games, keep your conversation civil and friendly. Even if the other fan persists in making annoying or unflattering remarks about your beloved team, don't take the bait. Simply smile and change the topic to a business issue.

Here are a few more conversation tips based on networking styles at sporting events:

Competitive Networkers. Don't take the winning or losing of your team too seriously.

Outgoing Networkers. Take care not to talk too much during play.

Amiable Networkers. Show a little bravado by letting the other person know sports-related activities that you currently play or at one time played well.

Analytical Networkers. Share your knowledge of the game or players without getting into a debate about which team or player is better.

Opening Lines at Sporting Events

"What did you think of the game?"

"What do you think about the upcoming match between . . . ?"

"I heard an interesting comment on TV last night about our team's coach."

"Do you like to play sports as much as you like to watch them?"

"What sports did you play as a kid?"

"Where do you get your sports news?"

Conversational Bridges to Business Topics

"I have a couple of friends in the sporting goods business. Are you in a business that is related to sports?"

"I have a small company that helps customers . . . ."

"I sell sports equipment to . . . ."

"If you know anyone who is looking for a personal trainer for . . . , I'm available."

"Do you know someone who can get me a good deal on . . . equipment?"

"I organize sporting events for corporate outings."

⃠ **Taboo Topics at Sporting Events** ⃠

✗ athletes using performance-enhancing drugs
✗ euthanasia in horse racing ✗ cheating ✗ betting
scandals ✗ gossip about athletes' personal lives
✗ badmouthing fans of other teams (beyond the normal
teasing and banter) ✗ talking about business for too long
✗ talking business if the other person prefers not to
✗ talking business during exciting moments

HIT A HOME RUN WHILE NETWORKING

In this chapter you've learned that sharing your passion for a professional sport can—if you don't get carried away—deepen relationships and create networking opportunities. You now know that after casually bringing up business issues at a sporting event, if you want to discuss them on a deeper level, then suggest to your companion that you meet either immediately or a few days after the event someplace where there are no distractions. Remember, the purpose of attending sporting events is to relax, have fun, and get to know each other better.

40

Live Performances

The English Puritan, William Prynne, once said, "Popular stage plays are sinful, heathenish, lewd, ungodly spectacles and the most pernicious corruption to the manner, minds and souls of men." On the other hand, the British lexicographer Samuel Johnson called music, "The only sensual pleasure without vice." George Bernard Shaw referred to dancing as, "A perpendicular expression of a horizontal desire." Live performers stimulating audiences' senses and emotions are among the many reasons why so many people love to talk and network with each other when they attend theater, music, plays, dance, and other live events.

The three primary opportunities for networking at live events are before the performance begins, during intermission, and after the program concludes. If you are a savvy networker, you will attempt to take advantage of at least one of these three opportunities. However, since the time you have to chat varies, if you want to transition to a business-related topic, do it quickly but tactfully so you don't appear as if you are prowling for customers or clients.

SOCIAL NETWORKS FOR MUSICIANS, ACTORS, DANCERS, AND OTHER PERFORMERS

These social networking sites offer great opportunities for bands, musicians, actors, dancers, and other performers to reach potential audiences and offer free or inexpensive listing services. Music-oriented sites offer resources for independent musicians, radio stations that will play your music, sites and publications that will review music, online services that sell MP3s and CDs, classifieds for musicians, and more. Actor- and dancer-oriented social networking sites offer listings for auditions, agents, competitions, performances, latest dances, career advice, schools, coaching, and more.

To find performing artists and related topics, type: *musicians (actors, dancers, etc.) + social networks* into your favorite search engine.

TOPICS THAT MOST NETWORKERS LIKE TO TALK ABOUT AT THEATER, MUSIC, AND DANCE PERFORMANCES

- Modern and classic playwrights, and plays
- Ballet, modern, and folk dancing
- New York, London, and regional theater
- Music, theater, and dance festivals
- Famous companies, theaters, and schools
- Famous musicians, stage actors, and dancers
- Performances, reviews, and recordings
- Performing arts business
- Sets, costumes, and lighting
- Travel, food, art, and culture

CONVERSATION TIP FOR ALL NETWORKING STYLES

Don't Publicly Pan a Performance

As I stepped into the theater lobby during intermission at a recent performance I couldn't help but hear a man bellow into his cell phone, "The show's nothing but a load of rubbish!" Everyone may be a critic, but voicing a negative opinion for everyone to hear at the performance is just bad manners. Plus, performers' family members may be within earshot and just imagine how an uncomplimentary review would make them feel—about you!

Opening Lines at Live Performances

"Do you have a preference when it comes to modern or classic plays?"

"I'm going to see a show next week by . . . ."

"What performances have you recently seen?"

"I always admired . . . . Who is your favorite?"

"Can you recommend a place to eat or get a drink after the show?"

Conversational Bridges to Business Topics

"I met a fellow in one of my workshops who produces plays. Since you are looking for investors in your play, do you want his telephone number?"

"I wonder if you know anyone in the theater business because I know a talented person who wants to get a job in that industry."

"I recently attended a business conference where one of the speakers said that many of the same concepts that apply to making a great performance also apply to running a successful enterprise. After seeing this show, I think I agree!"

$\bigcirc$ TABOO TOPICS AT THEATER, MUSIC AND DANCE PERFORMANCES $\bigcirc$

✗ critiquing a performance during intermission
✗ making snide comments about performers
✗ talking about who you'd rather see in a role
✗ making negative comparisons to past performances or to other performers

---

NETWORK AT PERFORMANCES TO FIND WHERE BUSINESS MEETS CULTURAL INTERESTS

In this chapter, you've learned that live performances can offer fertile networking opportunities because people who share cultural interests always have a lot to talk about. Now that you know how to segue from one discussion to another and then transition to related business topics, you will have time during intermission to find out where some of your cultural and business interests overlap with those of others attending the show.

41

Movie Theaters

You don't have to work in the film industry to network at the movies. Have you ever stood in line waiting to see a film and the person next to you says, "Have you seen any good movies lately?" You can bet that your conversation is just getting started and that networking won't be far behind. It is easy to segue from a conversation about a film and pop culture to many other business-related topics since there are so many careers, skills, and fields directly or indirectly related to this hugely popular industry.

Movies, like all pop culture, are a reflection of our society—past, present, and future, for better or worse—and therefore offer many opportunities and topics of conversation. People who like movies usually identify in some way with the stories and struggles of how "the good, the bad, and the ugly" cope with everyday problems and strive to succeed. And what could be more akin to networking than that?

> ### SOCIAL NETWORKS FOR PEOPLE WHO LOVE MOVIES OR WANT TO BE "IN THE BUSINESS"
>
> Social networking sites that feature movies offer users opportunities to share reviews, create top movie lists, post comments, and make friends with other fans or pros. Depending on the site, some offer movie lovers photos, news, ratings, previews, quizzes, showtimes—even the movies themselves! Local-oriented movie social networking groups also give users the opportunities to meet up with other film buffs and to chat about films and the network.
>
> To find other movie buffs, film professionals, and cinema-related activities, type: *film + movie career social networks* into your favorite search engine.

TOPICS THAT MOST NETWORKERS LIKE TO TALK ABOUT AT THE MOVIES

- Favorite actors and directors
- Latest films, reviews, Oscars, and festivals
- Film scores and scripts
- Movie business and industry news
- Best and worst movies
- Movie theaters
- Celebrity causes
- Movies and society
- Movie genres
- Performing arts

Here are a few conversation tips based on networking styles when talking to people at movies:

Competitive Networkers. If you don't like a film, avoid just bad-mouthing the movie's actors, writers, or other crew, even if they deserve it. Find something positive that you can comment on, too, so that it shows you can acknowledge the abilities of others.

Outgoing Networkers. Don't talk even a little bit during the film. Save your comments for after the movie, otherwise you'll annoy everyone around you.

Amiable Networkers. Don't be neutral when asked to share your opinions regarding the movies and actors. Neutral opinions suggest a lack of conviction or an unwillingness to take a position.

Analytical Networkers. Don't nitpick a film's technical short-comings. Bring out a scene or aspect of the movie you liked, so that you don't come across as someone overcritical who just focuses on "what's wrong."

Opening Lines to Talk to People at the Movies

"What did you think of his last movie?"
"My all-time favorite movie is . . . . What's yours?"
"What have you seen recently that you can recommend?"
"I just saw . . . and truly loved it."
"What kinds of movies do you like the best?"
"I'm particularly interested in . . . movies because . . . ."
"What's the weirdest movie you've seen recently?"
"Have you ever attended any film festivals?"
"Are you also interested in the other performing arts?"

Conversational Bridges to Business Topics

"I have a friend who is a filmmaker and teaches at a local college. If you're interested in learning more about moviemaking, I'll give you his e-mail."

"I'm in the catering business. We work with a lot of pro-
    duction companies when they are on shoots."
"I'm writing a screenplay about . . . ."
"I dreamed of becoming an actor when I was younger, but
    since I have no talent in that area I decided to become
    a . . . ."
"What line of work are you in?"
"I love movies, but I don't know anything about the film
    business. I'm in the . . . business. What about you?"

⃠ Taboo Topics at Movies ⃠

✗ exaggerating your experience in the film business
✗ panning the favorite actors and films of others
✗ pontificating about film and its impact on society
✗ telling how a film ends to someone who has not
        yet seen it ✗ discussing pornography

SMALL TALK AT THE MOVIES CAN LEAD TO MANY DIFFERENT BUSINESS DISCUSSIONS

You learned in this chapter that it's easy to strike up a conversation and make small talk at movies with other fans because films
touch on so many aspects of our lives. You now know that by listening carefully for keywords related to business—not just the
movie business, but any business—you can naturally transition
your conversations to more specific networking topics and be
closer to finding a big deal.

42

Museums

There was a time when visiting a museum seemed more like a walk though a cemetery—it was very quiet. However, today the popularity of museums has exploded, making them one of the best places to meet people and network. Whether you visit a museum that focuses on natural history, art, science and technology, or even rock and roll, breaking the ice, starting a conversation, and networking is easy because there are so many things to look at and talk about. In addition, people go to museums to learn about, see, and, in some cases, touch genuine and rare objects—things that they may have read about or seen in a book or film.

Many people who go to museums are willing to network with other visitors if they are properly approached. Asking a question, making a comment, or sharing some interesting information about an exhibit is the most natural way to make an initial connection with another visitor. Finding out and revealing the motivation for visiting the exhibit can lead to a more extended conversation and possibly a networking opportunity. Although many museum visitors are open to quietly chatting about the exhibits and revealing their personal or professional interests, respect the privacy of those who prefer to view the exhibitions without interruption.

A Night at the Museum and Social Networking!

What do you get when you combine social networking with the wild movie comedy *Night at the Museum* starring Ben Stiller? "Sleepover" programs at museums, zoos, and other tourist attractions all over the country that use social networks to publicize their events and sign up participants!

Some social networking sites for kids offer members access to programs such as the San Diego Zoo Wild Animal Park in Escondido, California's Beastly Bedtime and Roar and Snore sleepovers. They are designed for families with kids between the ages of 4 and 7. Another program hosted by the American Museum of Natural History in New York City presents a flashlight tour of either North American mammals or the dinosaur skeleton for kids between 8 and 12. Then the kids and adults sleep on cots in the Hall of Ocean Life, underneath the blue whale. While most of the social networking programs are geared for kids accompanied by an adult, some have expanded to adult programs, too. Whether you attend with a kid or by yourself, a museum overnighter is a great place to meet new people and network, even if your products or services do not directly relate to the exhibit.

> To find out more about the museums, related clubs, and activities in your area, type: *(your city)* + *museum* + *social networks* into your favorite search engine.

TOPICS THAT MOST NETWORKERS LIKE TO TALK ABOUT IN MUSEUMS

- Building design and construction
- Fund-raising and the business of art
- News about artists and curators
- Museum gifts and artifacts
- Lectures, exhibitions, and education
- Auctions and collectibles
- Performing arts and art classes
- *Antiques Road Show*
- Art history, natural history, science, society, and culture
- Artists' mediums, materials, and methods
- Art openings, galleries, and collecting
- Books and films about artists' lives
- Different kinds of museums

After breaking the ice with other museum visitors, here are some small-talk tips based on networking styles:

Competitive Networkers. Describe how an exhibit reinforces your motivation to achieve your business goals.

Outgoing Networkers. Ask others how the museum inspires their professional and personal interests.

Amiable Networkers. Describe how the exhibits give you ideas for your business.

Analytical Networkers. Share your interest in—not your opinion of—a particular exhibit and how it relates to your business.

Opening Lines at Museums

> "I wanted to see this exhibit because I'm planning on taking a trip to . . . ."
>
> "My favorite permanent display in this museum is the dinosaur exhibit. I'm an amateur paleontologist. What exhibits do you enjoy the most here?"
>
> "Do you have a background in art or art history (science and technology, history, etc.)?"
>
> "Have you tried the food in the museum restaurant? I hear it's pretty good."

Conversational Bridges to Business Topics

> "I'm involved in planning events for several of our city's cultural institutions, including . . . ."
>
> "What emerging artists do you recommend investing in?"
>
> "I dabble in collecting watercolors, but my main business is . . . ."
>
> "I work for another museum down the street. What about you? Are you in this business, too?"

⊘ Taboo Topics at Museums ⊘

✗ chatting up people who are obviously not interested in talking ✗ chattering loudly ✗ pontificating ✗ discussing business for too long while viewing the exhibits
✗ panning the exhibit or artist within earshot of others
✗ making impolite remarks about art or artists

DISCOVER HIDDEN BUSINESS TREASURES BY NETWORKING AT MUSEUMS

You have learned in this chapter what topics other people who go to museums like to talk about and how to engage them in business-related conversations. You now know that by encouraging others to talk about and share their impressions, feelings, goals, and dreams based on what they see at the museum, they will offer you insights into possible mutual business interests.

43

Nightclubs

Whether you enjoy dancing the night away to a pounding hip-hop beat or quietly sipping a drink while listening to a jazz trio, nightclubs have always been good places to meet people and network. If the atmosphere is cool and quiet, chatting and networking with someone seated near you will be easier than if the music is blaring so loud that it is nearly impossible to talk to or hear someone. However, in either situation, be sure to send out and look for receptive nonverbal signals such as smiling and eye contact.

Of course, many single people go to nightclubs to just have fun, meet people, and make friends. At the same time, many of these men and women are actively pursuing their careers, building their own businesses—some of which may be cutting edge—and striving for success in their companies, professions, and industries, thus making them great prospects as possible clients, customers, or networking contacts. Another benefit of networking in nightclubs is that people who enjoy evening entertainment often are open to chatting with other patrons about music, dancing, other aspects of pop culture, and their businesses.

SOCIAL NETWORKS FOR "NIGHTCLUB CRAWLERS"

If you are always on the lookout for the hottest nightclubs, then these social networks are the place to be. They allow users to share their passion for the music, dancing, hot spots, clothes, bands, and bling in the night club scene. DJs, live music, CD releases, "club crawls," and other promotions for industry fanatics and social network members who want to share their personal experiences, favorite dance music, clubs, videos, photos, and interests. These sites offer business resources for DJs, bands, music marketers, promoters, club owners, event planners, and others who want to become part of the industry or join the fun in the party scene.

To find nightclubs near you and people who enjoy discussing nightlife, type, *(your city)* + *social networks* + *nightclubs* + *(your interest)* into your favorite search engine.

TOPICS THAT MOST NETWORKERS LIKE TO TALK ABOUT IN NIGHTCLUBS

- Entertainment, nightlife, and lounges
- Pop culture, celebrities, and fast lifestyles
- Trendy and cheap restaurants
- Web sites and online communities
- Entrepreneurs and new businesses
- Bands, DJs, fans, CDs, and DVDs
- Theater, dance, and movies
- Computer games and online dating

- School, college, and careers
- Food, drink recipes, beer, and wine
- Hospitality businesses

CONVERSATION TIP FOR ALL NETWORKING STYLES

Dos and Don'ts for Singles Networking in Nightclubs

Don't use phony pickup lines, such as "Hey, didn't I see you on the cover of . . . ?"

Do break the ice with a positive comment, easy question, or by offering a sincere compliment.

Don't make comments about a person's physical appearance.

Do focus on the positive things others are wearing, doing, or saying.

Don't just talk about yourself.

Do show a sincere desire to learn what the person does for fun or a living.

Don't shout or scream over the music.

Do move closer to the other person so both of you can talk without shouting.

Don't be shy about changing the topic to business.

Do ask the other person for his or her contact information if you think there is a potential to help one another in some capacity.

Opening Lines at Nightclubs

"What other clubs do you like to go to?"

"Do you play a musical instrument?"

"My favorite club in town is . . . because I love the . . . ."

"That appetizer looks unusual. Do you mind me asking what it is?"

"What other clubs do you like to go to?"
"What is the strangest club you've been to?"

Conversational Bridges to Business Topics

"I like to come here after work for a drink and to listen to the music."

"I work in the . . . industry. What about you?"

"Since you said you are in the . . . business, can I ask you for some advice?"

"How do you keep your business growing?"

"If you were to do a completely different kind of work, what would it be?"

⊘ Taboo Topics in Nightclubs ⊘

✗ nightclub crimes ✗ war stories ✗ unpleasant news stories ✗ alcohol or substance-abuse, money, family, medical or personal problems ✗ sexual exploits ✗ sexually transmitted diseases ✗ abortion ✗ religious sects ✗ unkind personal comments ✗ eating disorders

---

NETWORKING IN NIGHTCLUBS MEANS BUSINESS

You learned in this chapter that if you network in nightclubs for new contacts and to forge business links, you need to keep your wits about you, especially as you sip drinks late into the evening. You now know that it is wise to treat this public networking situation for what it really is—a less structured and informal environment in which people interact, observe, and judge one another for their business potential.

44

Resorts

Where can you meet people from all over the world who you otherwise would not come in contact with, make new friends, and build a network of contacts—all the while surrounded by beautiful scenery and people having fun? Whether you are visiting or working at a ski, beach, or island resort, there are endless ways and opportunities to network for business, jobs, or just about anything else you might want or need.

Generally, resorts are full of energetic and friendly people who also enjoy traveling, socializing, and making connections for themselves and others. Maintaining contact with the people you meet at resorts can pay off big when it comes to business and networking, even if the opportunities don't come up right away. What's more important is that you shared a positive experience at the resort and that if and when opportunities do arise or you need a contact, you can call upon one another.

SOCIAL NETWORKING FOR TRAVELERS

Travel and lifestyle social networking communities are exploding all over the Internet and, with them, many opportunities to make social and business contacts. Though many travel social networking Web sites are designed for the leisure traveler, business travelers can use them, too. These travel sites allow members to keep track of all their contacts from around the world and facilitate meeting people who will be in the same place as you through online logs of your past, present, and future travels.

Members also see where their friends are and who is going where. At the same time, members can let others know their whereabouts, experiences, trip details, photos, and recommendations. In addition, several of these travel sites offer services such as e-mail, SMS, chatboards, instant messenger services, and an internal invite function to request a meeting. Why not? This approach to networking sure beats dining alone in your hotel room!

To learn more about particular resorts and their guests, type: *(resort) + (location) + guest reviews + travel social networks* into your favorite search engine.

TOPICS THAT MOST NETWORKERS LIKE TO TALK ABOUT WHEN AT RESORTS

- Hotels, casinos, and vacations spots
- Jobs in the hospitality and service industry
- Guests from around the world
- Cooking, ethnic food, and entertainment
- Cruises, tours, vacation packages, world travel, and adventure vacations

- Windsurfing, SCUBA diving, and other beach sports
- Conference and meeting facilities
- Unusual destinations
- Bareboat sailing and ocean cruising
- Bike and motorcycle tours
- Investments, retirement, and vacation homes
- Families, weddings, and anniversaries
- Travel industry
- Winter and mountain sports

CONVERSATION TIPS FOR ALL NETWORKING STYLES

Extending an Invitation at a Resort

Different networking styles respond to invitations, so adapt the phrasing of your invitation based on what you believe to be the person's networking style.

Competitive Networkers prefer the direct approach focused on an activity or game. For example, "Do you want to join us for a game of . . . ?"

Outgoing Networkers like being invited into activities, both large and small. "Why don't you come on over and join us. I'll introduce you to everyone."

Amiable Networkers are more comfortable accepting invitations to small group or one-on-one activities. For example, "Would you like to be my partner for this exercise?"

Analytical Networkers generally prefer accepting invitations to small, structured group activities. For example, you can ask, "We need a fourth person for our card game. Would you like to join us?"

Opening Lines at Resorts

"How do you like to spend your time when you're here?"

"I know some great places to eat around here. Would you like a few recommendations?"

"What would you recommend I should do if I have only three days?"

"What's the most interesting or unusual resort you've ever been to?"

"How did you find out about this resort?"

"Tell me a little bit about the place you stayed at when you visited . . . ."

Conversational Bridges to Business Topics

"What's it like working at this resort?"

"Do you know how I can get a job working at a place like this?"

"Our team won this vacation because we were the top moneymakers in the company."

"So you have a timeshare here? I've been thinking about buying one, too. Would you recommend it as a good investment?"

"I'm a chef so I'm always interested in what the food is like on cruise ships and at different resorts. What has been your experience with that?"

⊘ Taboo Topics at Resorts ⊘

✗ hard sell conversations ✗ loud chattering in quiet areas
✗ shop talk to uninterested parties
✗ economic woes ✗ business troubles ✗ world crisis
and war ✗ government policies ✗ local crime or
other negative news stories

MIX BUSINESS WITH PLEASURE WHEN YOU NETWORK AT RESORTS

You learned in this chapter that networking at resorts requires a keen sense of if, whether, when, and how to open a business conversation with other guests. You now know that rather than immediately launching into business discussions when you first meet, it's far better to engage others with plenty of small talk around nonbusiness-related topics. Then, when the opportunity arises, you can naturally segue to a business topic without appearing as though you are a networking shark trolling for clients.

45

Stores

"**A**ttention shoppers!" You probably visit a market, hardware store, bakery, dry cleaner, stationery store, salon, and many other places of business at least once a week. Now think of all the opportunities you have to network where you shop, particularly if your business is related to any one of the many products that fill today's boutiques, specialty food shops, malls, and department stores. Whether you offer products or services that can help these businesses be more productive and profitable, consider how they connect with some of the products or services available where you frequently shop. Because you regularly shop in particular establishments, you have an opportunity to not only network with the proprietors, managers, and staff, but also with other customers.

If you casually tailor your conversations to gently sharing your knowledge, experience, or expertise of particular products or services with other shoppers, you can increase store sales—something that every store manager and owner will certainly appreciate. As long as you do not intrude on the customers or interfere with the owner's or manager's way of doing business, networking where you shop will not be a problem.

SOCIAL NETWORKING FOR PEOPLE WHO LOVE TO SHOP

If you want to network for customers or vendors, or learn more about retail trends then shopping-oriented social networks are the places to be. Online social shopping communities are where people discover, recommend, and share products. These sites allow users to organize their shopping through lists by product, price, gifts, and people. Community members can create and join groups, share advice, feedback, offer product suggestions, get discounts on popular products, and find the best prices. Members can personalize their profiles so they can discover new products from people with similar styles. Part social-networking club, part pop–business culture incubator, these online style clubs are for people who live for fashion, design, and shopping and who want to have their finger on the pulse of trendsetting businesses.

To find stores near you that carry your favorite products, type: *(your city) (product)* + *shopping social networks* into your favorite search engine.

TOPICS THAT MOST NETWORKERS LIKE TO TALK ABOUT IN STORES

- Housewares and appliances
- Gourmet foods, cooking, and entertaining
- Home improvement and decorating

- Related retail businesses
- Store staff and customer service
- Sales, merchandising, and display
- Restaurants and entertainment
- Families, schools, and lifestyles
- Holiday sales and seasonal promotions
- Advertising and promotion
- Special in-store events and demonstrations
- Small businesses and entrepreneurs
- New products
- Frequent buyer programs
- Customer incentives
- Other customers
- Swap meets, flea markets, and yard sales
- Store competitors

CONVERSATION TIPS FOR ALL NETWORKING STYLES

Three Ways to Connect with Other Shoppers

Since many enjoy shopping, it's a great place to meet people. Here are three ways to quickly connect with others in the store.

1. *Display approachable and friendly body language.* People are more willing to open a conversation with you if you smile, make eye contact, and keep your arms uncrossed. If you see a friendly looking person shopping in the same area as you, take the initiative, say hello, and ask an easy-to-answer question about a product around you.
2. *Be conversational and easy to talk to.* Enjoy the moment and let the other person know you are hav-

ing fun talking to him or her. Be informal, friendly, and animated. Ask questions and talk about fashion, clothes, food, or whatever else you are shopping for.

3. *Share a shopping tip, favorite food, recipes, or if asked, your opinion.* Depending on the store, tell the other person what area or products you like the best. If he or she asks your opinion about a possible clothing purchase, answer tactfully. Most people want opinions regarding their appearance that reinforce, not contradict, their own views.

Opening Lines in Stores and Places You Shop

"I see you shopping here all the time, too! This is a great place, isn't it?"

"This store is my favorite place to shop for . . . . What do you come here for?"

"I don't work here but I know this place like the back of my hand. Do you need some help?"

"Excuse me, but you look like you know about . . . and I'm afraid I'm a novice. What would you recommend that I buy for a gift in the range of about $. . . ?"

Conversational Bridges to Business Topics

"I like to look at different stores to see their displays and how they merchandise their products because I'm in this business, too. What do you think of this?"

"I shop here because they have the best produce. I run a restaurant in the neighborhood so I'm always looking for what's fresh in the market when I'm planning the daily menu."

"Do you have a professional interest in these kinds of products?"

"What are some of the trends you see in the . . . business?"

"What styles are hot with the . . . these days?"

"What advice would you give someone looking to open a retail store that sells . . . ?"

"I'm looking for a consultant who can help me choose the right . . . . Can you recommend someone?"

⊘ Taboo Topics at Stores ⊘

✗ spending more time networking in a store than shopping ✗ offering unsolicited advice to other shoppers ✗ monopolizing the time of customers or staff ✗ staring into people's carts showing too much interest in what they are buying ✗ discussing with store staff alternate possibilities for employment ✗ pressuring shoppers to buy anything ✗ suggesting customers take their business elsewhere

---

NETWORKING, SHOPPING, AND BIG DEALS GO TOGETHER

In this chapter you learned that you can "go shopping for contacts" as well as bargains. You now know that serendipity plays a role when your objective is to connect with other shoppers and that small talk can naturally transition into networking about mutual business interests, and maybe even into big deals.

46

Waiting Rooms

"Who's next?" Hurry up and wait—that's pretty much the rule when it comes to doctor and dentist appointments. Yet, along with all that waiting, there are opportunities to network with other patients seated in the waiting rooms. Of course, most people visit doctors, dentists, and other medical practitioners because they or someone they are with has an illness, condition, or problem that needs attention. Therefore, exercise an extra dose of tact when it comes to discussing health issues, and don't be surprised or offended if the other person doesn't share details or reasons behind his or her medical visit. That's natural and, of course, good manners dictate respecting the person's right to privacy.

However, if the situation presents itself, why not see if the person next to you is interested in having a conversation? After all, there are plenty of other topics that you can bring up without touching on a sensitive medical issue and, besides, chatting about common interests is a great way to pass the time. Also, if you visit the doctor on a regular basis, look for others who are usually there at the same time as you. They may be people with whom you can network whenever you see them since familiarity leads to trust and rapport.

SOCIAL NETWORKS FOR SHARING MEDICAL RESEARCH, STRUGGLES, INFORMATION, AND TREATMENTS

Medical social networks are useful for patients, health-care professionals, service providers, and vendors. They focus on health and wellness by providing members with health-care data and information, community programs, and recent advances in a wide variety of medical, psychological, and life conditions areas. Patient-oriented communities offer members feedback, forums, referrals, and support groups. Medical social networks used by health-care professionals allow members to manage institutional knowledge, disseminate peer-to-peer knowledge, and highlight and/or screen individual physicians and institutions.

In addition, members can find professional contacts with common interests, gain referrals, increase their visibility within their area of expertise, recruit patients for clinical trials, stay informed of the latest medical advancements, keep in touch with former colleagues and graduate/medical school classmates, and communicate with advanced health professionals around the world.

To find out more about careers or trends in the medical industry or other related topics, type: *medical careers + social networks* or *health-care professional + patient social networks* into your favorite search engine.

TOPICS THAT MOST NETWORKERS LIKE TO TALK ABOUT IN WAITING ROOMS

- Books, magazine, and newspaper articles
- Business trends and technology
- Dieting, health, and homecare
- Eastern medical practices
- Clues in crossword and Sudoku puzzles
- Travel and leisure
- Celebrity news
- Herbal medicines and treatment
- Doctor referrals

CONVERSATION TIPS FOR ALL NETWORKING STYLES

Six Comments You Should Never Make to Another Patient in a Doctor's Office

Since most people feel anxious or uncomfortable while in a doctor's waiting room, insensitive or tactless comments can have an even more negative impact than usual. Therefore *never* say:

1. "You think what you've got is bad, just listen to this!"
2. "Well, according to what I've read, there goes your sex life."
3. "Gosh, I thought they cured that disease a long time ago."
4. "I hope this doctor knows what he's doing."
5. "I have a friend who had the same problem as you and she's not doing too well."
6. "Have you ever considered having those moles removed?"

Opening Lines in Waiting Rooms

> "I see that you're reading that article on the newest medical treatment for . . . . Was it interesting?"
>
> "I couldn't help but notice that you are here every Wednesday, too. Have you been a patient of Dr. . . . for a long time?"
>
> "I'm curious, what's that article say about . . . ?"
>
> "I like the staff here. They are professional, but they really seem to care about their patients."

Conversational Bridges to Business Topics

> "I can see from your briefcase that you work for . . . company. How do you like working for that company?"
>
> "What would you say are the biggest changes affecting your business and sales?"
>
> "Since you work in . . . . I know a company that you might be interested in contacting because . . . "
>
> "I like the way the secretary handled that client. We're all in the customer service business!"
>
> "Are you in the medical field?"
>
> "Speaking of business, I just read an interesting article about . . . ."
>
> "Now that the baby boomers are starting to retire, I'm interested in the business of . . . ."
>
> "Medical insurance is so complicated! I read about a company that helps people complete the insurance forms and navigate the system. I'd like to invest in that company!"

$\bigcirc$ Taboo Topics in Waiting Rooms $\bigcirc$

✕ medical horror stories ✕ malpractice suits ✕ hospital
and doctor mistakes ✕ negative comments about doctors
and the medical industry ✕ insurance fraud ✕ doctor
shortages ✕ doctor jokes ✕ complaining about doctor's
fees ✕ telling the doctor or health practitioner how
to do his or her job ✕ accusing the doctor or staff
of making a mistake ✕ threatening to switch doctors
or report them to the medical licensing board
✕ criticizing a doctor's colleague

MAKING SMALL TALK IN WAITING ROOMS
CAN OPEN NETWORKING DOORS

In this chapter you learned that if you get a positive response
from someone while chatting in a waiting room, it can be profitable to share some "free information" about your business or
industry. You now know that if someone asks you questions or
discloses business-related information, it may be the first step
that opens the door to networking and business opportunities.

CONCLUSION

Hurrah! You're ready to turn small talk into big deals every day, no matter where you are, what you are doing, or with whom you are speaking. You have learned hundreds of opening lines, networking strategies, goals, and key things to do to make profitable connections before and during business and social events, and even in public places. You also now know how to meet people and make small talk while working a room, overcome shyness, use impromptu speaking to build your professional image, and escape people at networking events who waste your time. Finally, you have learned several specific ways to build lasting business relationships and correct the most common networking mistakes.

In the end, your success at networking and turning small talk into big deals hinges on your ability to connect, build rapport, and establish relationships with the people you meet in professional, social, and public situations. So now it is up to you to turn the information you learned in this book into practical results. I promise that if you follow my recommendations with a focused and consistent approach to strategic networking, you will turn almost every conversation and encounter into a rewarding and beneficial experience for all those you meet.

Index

About the Author

Don Gabor is an author, a communications trainer, and a small-talk expert. He has written eight books, including the bestseller, *How to Start a Conversation and Make Friends*. His books have been translated into 13 languages.

Gabor trains executives, managers, and staff on how to communicate more effectively with coworkers and clients. He has been presenting his programs to Marriott hotels, Time-Warner, Korin Japanese Trading Corp., and many other companies, businesses, and organizations since 1980. He founded his company, Conversation Arts Media, in 1991.

For individuals who want one-on-one training, Gabor also offers executive coaching for English oral and written skills, public speaking, workshop presentation, networking, and media training.

Gabor is a member of the National Speakers Association. He was a media spokesperson for Sprint, Frito-Lay, and Grand Marnier and is a frequent media guest. He has been featured in hundreds of television, radio, and print interviews, including *60 Minutes with Andy Rooney. The New Yorker* called Gabor "a gifted conversationalist."

For more information about Don Gabor's books, training programs, and free conversation tip sheets, please visit his Web site at www.dongabor.com.

You can also contact him at 718-768-0824,
via e-mail at don@dongabor.com, or via snail mail at:
Don Gabor
P.O. Box 715
Brooklyn, NY 11215